P9-BZV-809

LINCOLN CHRISTIAN COLLEGE AND SEMINARY

Escaping the Time Crunch

Escaping

THE
TIME
CRUNCH

MARK LITTLETON

MOODY PRESS
CHICAGO

© 1990 by
Mark R. Littleton

All rights reserved.
No part of this book may be reproduced
in any form without permission in writing
from the publisher, except in the case of brief
quotations embodied in critical articles or reviews.

All Scripture quotations, unless noted otherwise,
are from the *Holy Bible: New International Version*.
Copyright © 1973, 1977, 1984, International Bible Society.
Used by permission of Zondervan Bible Publishers.

The use of selected references from various versions
of the Bible in this publication does not necessarily imply
publisher endorsement of the versions in their entirety.

ISBN: 0-8024-2292-6

1 2 3 4 5 6/BC/Year 94 93 92 91 90

Printed in the United States of America

*To Grandpop and Grandmom Littleton
who always had time enough
for the things that counted*

97204

Contents

Introduction: The Hurry Scurry Society   11

Part 1: The Problem: "Tired Is My Middle Name"

1. God: What on Earth Does He Want from Me?   21
2. The Church: Meetinged Out   27
3. Me: Too Much to Do,
      Too Little Time to Do It In   37
4. The Family: Hurry Sweet Hurry   47
5. Work: 40 Hours Just Doesn't Cut It!   53

Part 2: Answers: The Divine Line on Time

6. Choose This Day Whom You Will Serve   63
7. The Days Are Evil   73
8. A Time for Everything Under the Sun   87
9. God's Goals   95
10. We Are His Workmanship   103
11. Priorities Made in Heaven   113
12. Redeeming the Time   125
13. Don't Worry, Be Joyful   135

Part 3: Choices: Where the Battle Is Won or Lost

14. Your Kingdom or God's?   153
15. Vacillating Interest or Valued Intimacy?   161

16. Things on Earth or Treasure in Heaven?   169
17. Playing Around or Plowing Forward?   175
18. Productivity or People?   185
19. Temporal Ease or True Rest?   195
20. Frustration or Freedom?   207
21. Quantity or Quality?   217
22. Jack of All Trades or Master of One?   227

Part 4: The Battle Can Be Won

23. Conclusion: Take Time to Dance   235

Time

Just a few questions.

When the Creator wound up the earthly clock,
did He just let it go,
or did He plan each tock?

If I ended today, say time ran out,
would I still be somewhere in time
stumbling about?

When eternity begins and time ceases to be,
will we tell time in heaven,
or will we just swing free?

How come no matter how much time I save,
my boss scrutinizes his stopwatch
then begins to rant and rave?

Why is it that if I hustle and run,
time only goes faster
than a son of a gun?

This last one I know isn't especially deep,
but when I wake up why do I feel
like I just fell asleep?

Well, there they all are sitting right on the page;
can you give me some answers,
or should I just act my age?

Introduction
The Hurry Scurry Society

*I greatly enjoyed reviewing the cover of the May issue,
"Time Out! Life on the Run Takes Its Toll." Unfortunately, I haven't yet had time to stop and read it.*
> —Thomas J. Wiens, letter to the
> editor, *Moody Monthly*, after publi-
> cation of their article on the time
> crunch, May 1989

Tired is my middle name.
> —Carol Rohder, *Time*, April 24, 1989

John F. Kennedy presided over Camelot. Lyndon
Baines Johnson launched "The Great Society." Now
President Bush has spoken of the "thousand points of
light."

In light of modern-day conditions, that phrase
might better be, "The thousand flickering, fleeting, flying, and dying pulsations of light." Or, to parody President Johnson, "The Hurry Scurry Society."

Time no longer just ticks. It crunches. It squeezes
people from waking to retiring until they literally feel
like a used toothpaste tube.

You see it all over. It used to be commuters read
newspapers on the train. Now you see them reading in
their cars—while driving. They glance up at the road occasionally and veer out of the way of oncoming trucks,
then go back to the headlines.

People eat breakfast, lunch, and dinner in their cars. You find the refuse in the back seat. My wife told me about a friend's car, "Mark, it's a garbage scow. They must eat and sleep in the thing."

We now have car phones. But not to gossip. Some of the deals of the hour are made while stalled in traffic on Route 95. It won't be long before we have bike phones and even personal "belt phones." Captain Kirk's "Beam me up, Scotty" on "Star Trek" of some years ago will become a reality.

At health clubs people ride stationary cycling machines. But they're not bent over the handlebars. They're peering over a stack of reports, memos, and spread sheets. "I do some of my best work on the Nautilus equipment," one man says. "Build your business while you build your body, I say."

Families rarely sit down together to partake of a finely cooked repast. They're lucky if they cross paths on the way to the microwave. And all those home conveniences haven't made home anything more than a convenience. Some developments are called "bedroom communities." The only time Papa Bear, Mama Bear, and Baby Bear are there is to cut some Z's.

NO TIME FOR INTIMACY

But it gets worse. Faith W. Brigel, a licensed clinical social worker in Palo Alto, California, works with women's groups to help them cope with the time crunch. She said, "We're not in the '60s and '70s any more. The '80s are a time of working hard and accumulating as much as you can. It's hectic. It's frantic. There's no time for intimacy; there's no closeness."[1]

The work world has changed dramatically. A recent Harris poll cited some startling statistics: in 1973 we worked an average of 40.6 hours per week. In 1987 it was up to 46.8.

At the same time, leisure hours took a nose dive—down from 26.2 hours weekly to 20.2. That's six hours less for wife, kids, and everything else we do that matters to us and our Lord. Other Harris surveys show that professionals work 52.2 hours weekly, and small business people normally log 57.3 hours a week.[2]

What's the cause of all this activity? Experts cite a number of factors. One is the increased competition from abroad that businesses in the U.S. have encountered. Everyone has to put in more time to make ends meet.

A second concerns our movement from a manufacturing to a service economy. When you're in the service sector, you're at everyone's beck and howl.

Strangely, a third comes from federal regulations. The sheer quantity of paperwork that businesses, doctors, and lawyers have to fill out is enormous.[3]

WORKING MOTHERS

The number of working mothers also contributes greatly to the time crunch people are feeling. An article in the *Wall Street Journal*[4] cites some new Census Bureau Statistics that indicate this. Sixty-five percent of mothers with children under eighteen work, compared with 64.7 percent last year. Fifty point eight percent of mothers with newborns were likely to be found on the job. And working mothers of preschoolers has remained constant at 56 percent. More mothers on the job means less time in the home, less time building the castle, less time for "quality" relationships.

A Boston University group headed up by Bradley Googins and Diane Burde surveyed 1,600 employees at a public utility and a high-tech company. Thirty-six percent of fathers and 37 percent of mothers said they felt "a lot of stress" trying to keep work and family life in balance.[5]

There's just not enough time to go around, let alone get around.

THE CHURCH SOMETIMES ADDS TO THE BURDEN

You'd think in the midst of all this that the church would offer us a haven in the hurry.

It's not always so. Tim Kimmel, president of Generation Ministries, works especially with young people and their parents. He says the time crunch is a combination of factors. But there's a definite "lure in the hurried life-style." Many of us find a strange neurotic solace in the fact that our days are jam-packed, our schedules bursting, and our lives spilling away weeks at a shot. Kimmel told me, "The media exploits it. Business rewards it. Our egos demand it. And even the church encourages it. The church can actually be part of the problem. We demand that people be involved—Sunday morning, Sunday night, Wednesday night. And if you're not, you're probably not really spiritual. We often equate spirituality with activity." Frenetic activity!

Gene Getz, well-known author and the mentor behind the Center for Church Renewal in Plano, Texas, agrees. "People are being pulled in many different directions. There's school. There's the competitiveness in the workplace. Working mothers. The economic burden. Sure, there's some materialism and some necessity. But in many cases it really takes two salaries to live."

Does the church contribute to the problem?

Sometimes—but not always—it does. Getz has this to say about the churches that do: "Well, we teach people to devote time to the family. Then we fill up the church schedule until it's overloaded. People have to make choices about what meetings they can attend. And then we tell them they have to be committed to the Lord. The real tension spreads when we want people to be more involved. That confronts them with more choices. And the guilt level goes up."

Randy Schiller, a computer consultant in Baltimore, Maryland, asserts that the problem for him is that "people ask you to do things in the church, and once you get

going you feel tremendous inner pressure not to quit.
You feel there's no one there to take your place. The
guilt goes up."

PERSONALLY

As a baby boomer of average proportions, I know
the time-crunched feeling well. Why just yesterday I
caught myself doing six things at once. I was reading
the *Wall Street Journal* while talking to my wife on the
phone while munching on my morning doughnut, all
the while watching the computer to make sure the
printout was clean, checking the calendar to be sure of a
date, and writing a thought down in my handy-dandy
pocket secretary. (Oh, what I wouldn't do for a real one!)

Before that I left my home, having made my instant
coffee by filling the cup with "hot" water from the tap. I
can't stand waiting for the pot to boil! And I was doing
that thinking that I'd get to work thirty seconds sooner
so I could catch up on some Scripture reading before I
waded into the day. But lo and behold—disaster struck.
My bowels made a demand, and I lost even more than
thirty seconds in the bathroom. So much for my Scripture reading!

I tend to plan my day while traveling from my desk
to the secretary's station. "That's dead time," I tell myself. "I can use it to think a little." Sometimes I even
pray for a need to visit the men's room just so I can get a
few minutes to myself!

Vacations? Forget it. I just want to lie in bed so that
I can prepare myself for the next thirteen weeks of the
rat careen. It used to be called a "race." No more.
There's no longer a direction or a goal. It's just go, go,
go. Where? Anywhere, so long as you're breathing hard
and churning up dust.

Some folks I know have been reduced to . . .

> cutting their showers so that they do their backs
> on Mondays, the feet on Tuesdays, and a rinse

only every third day (underarms, every day, of course—they do have some respect left for others),

eating dinner while reading the paper, exhorting their children to finish their dinners, and grunting at anything the wife says,

using car time to listen to a tape, meditate on Scripture, write down pertinent ideas, and cram a burger into their mouths all at once,

making dates to visit friends so they can say at least they tried, then canceling at the last minute because . . . well, no real reason (just wrung out, I guess), and

ripping through paperwork—literally.

You ask, "Are they kidding?" Only part time.

You ask, "Isn't this sin?" We plead the seven o'clock news on that one.

You ask, "Do you like your life?" What's there to like? Most of us haven't watched it long enough to feel it go by.

Still, we know we're not the only ones. Maybe you're in the same fix. Or fax.

Did I say fax? Now there's a time saver. Only problem is that after you fax something, you usually receive something back. And it'll probably be eighteen more pages than you sent! Then you'll have to find time to respond to it, copy it for others, file it, put it on the hard disk, and on, and on.

Is This the Way God Intended It?

Did God intend that our lives be this way? If so, how then could He say, "Be still, and know that I am God" (Psalm 46:10)? Or, "The Lord is my shepherd, I shall not want. He makes me lie down in green pastures, he leads me beside the quiet waters, he restores my soul" (Psalm 23:1-2)? He might have better said, "The Lord is my fast-track coach, I shall get what I want. He makes me get up and go; He leads me through the quiet waters in my all-terrain vehicle; He gets me to the store."

Ah, the good life.

The good life?! This is good?

To answer my question, no, God doesn't intend our lives to be this way. There is hope. In the course of this book I'll give you some ideas, some principles, and some Scripture on the subject. These are things I myself have applied in recent days, and I know they work. I'd like to help you get out of the time crunch and into something far more comfortable. In fact, I'll try to keep each chapter short. Each one will be less than . . .

Well, let's not make promises we can't keep. But this one thing I do promise: if you read this book at the rate of one page a minute, you can be done just in time . . .

to answer that fax, take a shower (and even do your back), grunt something at the wife, straighten your collar, write down a thought in your pocket secretary, and catch a headline out of the corner of your eye as you listen to the morning news.

Right?

NOTES

1. Claudia Morain, "The Stress of Having It All, *Washington Post*, July 11, 1988, p. C5.

2. Joan Libman, "Heigh-Ho, Heigh-Ho, It's Off to Work . . . " *Washington Post*, July 11, 1988, p. C5

3. Ibid.

4. "Are Working Mothers a Trend That's Peaked?" *Wall Street Journal*, November 2, 1988, p. B1.

5. Cathy Trost, "Men, Too, Wrestle with Career-Family Stress," *Wall Street Journal*, November 1, 1988, p. B1

Part 1

The Problem: "Tired Is My Middle Name"

1

God: What on Earth
Does He Want from Me?

*"You have planted much, but have harvested little.
You eat, but never have enough. You drink, but never
have your fill. You put on clothes, but are not warm.
You earn wages, only to put them in a purse with
holes in it. . . . Why?" declares the Lord Almighty.
"Because of my house, which remains a ruin, while
each of you is busy with his own house."*

—Haggai 1:6, 9

For years I have used a quote from Martin Luther
when speaking on the subject of prayer. "I have so
much to do today, I'll have to spend the first three hours
in prayer or the devil will get the victory."

So much to do?

The devil will get the victory?

The first *three hours* in prayer?!

Yikes! If that's what Martin Luther—whose accomplishments and biographies take up more space on library shelves than those of any other human besides
Jesus—had to do, what about me? Is the devil getting
the victory every day?

Frankly, that quote doesn't empower me to pray
more; it nearly embalms me. Three hours in prayer?
The first three? Before he even tore through the paperwork? Before he even put out the brush fires?

Now I know I'm a complete goof!

HAVE YOU EVER FELT THAT WAY?

Have *you* ever felt that way—like a Christian "goof"? Like you're just not cutting it, not living up to what God wants or expects?

Discipleship Journal recently carried an article titled "I Don't Feel Like a Very Good Christian."[1] The article begins with an illustration of a wife who was quieter than usual one evening. When her husband asked her what was wrong, she said, "I don't feel like a very good Christian."

What was the reason for her problem? She replied, "I haven't had a quiet time for a while. After chasing two small kids all day, I feel wiped out; I'm too tired to read the Bible and pray. Mornings are crazy, and the kids don't nap at the same time, so I haven't had devotions in weeks. I'm not even sure I have a relationship with God anymore."

That lady was suffering from what I call the "Quiet Time Guilt Syndrome." Usually it means that if you miss your quiet time one day, the Lord simply brushes it off. If you miss two, He grimaces and bends over the clouds, gazing sternly upon the roof of your house. And if you miss three, well, you'll find examples of what happens in the book of Revelation.

You may think I'm joking. Really, I'm not. There are many committed Christians who look at it that way.

Still, the problem can get far worse. Ever find yourself saying any of the following?

"I'm not using my gifts as much as I should."

"I told him no, and I feel absolutely terrible."

"The class went well, but I don't feel so good about it. I only spent forty-five minutes preparing for it this week."

"I just don't think I can ever please God the way I should."

"If I'm not doing something spiritual, I feel as though I'm wasting God's time and my life."

Are these outlooks true?

THE SCRIPTURES ARE CLEAR

The Scriptures are clear on the issue. They tell us to "redeem the time" (see Ephesians 5:15-17, KJV*), to "make the most of every opportunity" (Colossians 4:5-6), to be ready to preach the word "in season and out of season" (2 Timothy 4:2), and to "number our days" so that we can present to God "a heart of wisdom" (Psalm 90:12).

But somehow our fallen psyches can twist all those truths until they become a monstrous burden. Just what is it to "redeem the time"? Are we supposed to fill up every minute with spiritual pursuits?

How do we "make the most" of every opportunity? What if opportunity knocks and we aren't ready? Will the Lord give us a swift kick for that foul-up when we stand before His judgment seat?

As for preaching the word and witnessing, most of us know the frustration of that one. "I do well just to keep from offending people by my normal personality, let alone with the gospel," one man says. Many don't share their faith one time in a year, let alone "in season and out of season."

And that one about "numbering our days" sounds too much like "your days are numbered." Which we all feel acutely.

THE COMMON DENOMINATOR

Guilt is what's common in all those statements. If we use our time well, we feel guilty about the minute we wasted savoring a cup of coffee. If we don't use our time

* King James Version.

well, we feel doubly guilty. And if we use our time well and don't feel guilty, some well-meaning Christian is bound to say something that wipes us out anyway!

Part of the problem is that we just don't know what pleases God. Does His program allow for leisure, wasting time, sitting and staring, and a good video game? Or do we have to so seek his kingdom and righteousness that every minute must be jam-packed with spirituality? Just what does God want from us?

REASONS FOR THE "I'M A LOUSY CHRISTIAN" SYNDROME

If your time crunch relates to guilt and feeling like you're not pleasing God, welcome to the club. Martin Luther went through so many depressions and battles with the devil about pleasing God, he once hurled a filled inkwell at the wall in frustration. Tourists can still ogle those ink blotches.

A. W. Tozer wrote that "Satan's first attack upon the human race was his sly effort to destroy Eve's confidence in the kindness of God. . . . Nothing twists and deforms the soul more than a low or unworthy conception of God."[2]

What are the reasons we feel we can never please God in our use of time?

One is misinterpreting His Word. If we think that "redeeming the time" means filling it up and packing each minute with as much spiritual wallop as we can, we'll never cease to be frustrated. But if we want to gain a sense of joy and hope in the Christian life, we must know whereof the Word speaks. We can only worship Him in spirit and "in truth."

A second is giving God characteristics He doesn't possess. If we think of God as an ogre staring down over the balustrades of heaven looking for someone having fun so that He can beat him with His mace, we've got an impression that can't help but dent the spirit. Yet, how many Christians feel that no matter how much they do, it isn't enough for God? What does that make Him but a workaholic heavenly Boss who demands the same of His employees?

A third is the tendency to compare our own achievements with those of other Christians. You'll always find someone who appears to be doing more than you. I recently read about Paul Yongghi Cho, pastor of the largest church on earth. He prays five hours every day. *Five hours! Every day!* I have to admit, that doesn't stir me; it flattens me. If that's what we have to do to please God, most of us would be lucky to make it once in a lifetime.

IT SEEMS TO ME . . .

Our problem with time and God may be boiled down to several questions:

1. Just what does God expect of us in our use of time?

2. What is true failure in the matter of time in God's eyes?

3. What principles has He given us in the Word to help us please Him?

Understanding the answers to those questions is what we'll consider in the next two sections. But for now, let's leave the questions open. Our problem is bigger than simply our relationship with the Lord, though that is big enough.

We also have problems in the church.

NOTES

1. Kevin A. Miller, "I Don't Feel Like a Very Good Christian," *Discipleship Journal*, no. 47 (1988), p. 6.

2. A. W. Tozer, "A God Who Is Easy to Please," *Discipleship Journal*, no. 47 (1988), p. 10.

2

The Church: Meetinged Out

The church, not the world, should be the pacesetter.
—Robert H. Surpless, letter to the
editor, *Moody Monthly,* May 1989

When I wrote an article on the time crunch for *Moody Monthly* in May 1989, Robert H. Surpless responded with a letter to the editor. He wrote, "Littleton paints the church as a victim of life's pressures. The Bible and experience picture it as a refuge. The church, not the world, should be the pacesetter by keeping its Sunday evening and Wednesday services alive and well attended through Spirit-filled ministry."[1]

I don't disagree with Mr. Surpless's words. The church shouldn't be a victim of life's pressures. It should be "the pacesetter." Above all it should feature "well-attended services" that are characterized by "Spirit-filled ministry."

BUT WHAT IF . .

But what if it isn't a pacesetter? What if it's sitting back in the crowd running behind leaders who clearly are running in the ruts of the world? And what if the services aren't characterized by "Spirit-filled ministry" but by

poorly prepared sermons,
poorly executed music and specials,

leadership that is unclear about its goals and purpose,

twenty percent of the people doing all the work, and the rest just looking on,

a general lack of enthusiasm about anything spiritual,

an attitude that would rather sleep in than go to services,

a steady piling on of guilt about not doing enough, not serving enough, not participating enough,

a pastor working seventy to eighty hours a week with no end in sight?

If that's your church, it's bound to make people feel confused, angry, and unwilling to give their time and effort to the ministry.

PLEASE UNDERSTAND

I'm not condemning the modern church or saying that all churches come under the above description. Far from it. Clearly, there are many strong, Spirit-filled leaders and churches out there.

But there are others that are not. Some of them are like the Laodicean church of Revelation 3:14-22. Look at verses 15 to 17: "I know your deeds, that you are neither cold nor hot. I wish you were either one or the other! So, because you are lukewarm—neither hot nor cold—I am about to spit you out of my mouth. You say, 'I am rich; I have acquired wealth and do not need a thing.' But you do not realize that you are wretched, pitiful, poor, blind and naked."

HOW IS IT AFFECTING THE CHURCH?

Just the same, as dismal as the situation appears, what may be even worse is the impact of the time crunch on the church.

Michael Green, associate professor of field education at Dallas Theological Seminary, comments on the low attendance we see in many churches: "Sunday evening in many churches is dead. Wednesday night prayer meeting is a ghost. It's impossible to maintain these programs in many churches."

Notice the emphasis, though, on "many." Not all. Not even most. But does that mean we should shut down services?

Not necessarily. Simply cutting back because the services aren't packed out doesn't mean the "faithful few" shouldn't be nourished.

What is clear is that only quality programs and ministries will attract the average saint. If he doesn't get anything out of it, why put anything into it? Granted, that "what's in it for me" outlook is sinful. But if we can't get them to listen to the message, how can we teach them the truth of our own sinfulness?

Sometimes the church is "the last one to figure out what's going on," adds Tim Kimmel. And that's tragic, because the family is already under pressure from other sources. "The whole system punishes the traditional family," Kimmel observes. "The school system abuses them. The government offers them no tax breaks. And the church takes advantage of the 'nice' folks who can't seem to say no. Then they burn out."

THE DISAPPEARANCE OF THE VOLUNTEER

Women used to be a mainstay of the church's structure. They had the time and could volunteer to help out where the men couldn't. No more. "They were available to provide unbudgeted labor," Green says. "Now the church not only has to hire a youth pastor and a minister of Christian education, but someone to do the women's ministries, the children's ministries. It's becoming more professional—less of a servant atmosphere."

Ramona Tucker, an editor with Harold Shaw Publishers, has worked with teens for nearly six years; her husband has been involved for ten. They have recently pulled out for personal reasons. She commented, "One problem is that many wives' husbands don't even come to church. That's one pressure. Then the younger wives with small children only want to work with groups that have their children. After that you have older women who feel they gave their part in their younger years, and now the young women should be doing the main work. It's getting so churches simply have to hire people to do everything."

Worse!

But the cry for something to "meet my needs" has even hit the very heart of the ministry, the pastor's home. A pastor's wife said, "I'm involved in a Bible study at *another* church. I was leading one in my husband's church, but it wasn't fulfilling. I wanted people to get to know the Lord better. But the group wanted to go in another direction. So I found a group in another church that desired that." If pastor's wives are bailing out, what hope is there for the rest of us?

Eileen Merrell and her husband, Mike, of Silver Spring, Maryland, serve as Sunday school teachers and teen counselors. But they had to cut back on the counseling due to time pressures. She added, "I pray it is not a permanent situation."

Clearly, fewer women are able to devote the time and effort they once had.

Radical Social Transition

Another factor adding to the time crunch is the radical social transition of the past few years. It has affected the church dramatically. There are more working mothers, single parents, divorcées, stepfamilies, and people with nontraditional sexual orientations than ever before. All this has affected the family's role in the church.

The result is that some Christians are even taking refuge *from* the church. They're refusing to go to all the meetings in favor of having a fairly normal family life at home.

What people lament even more is the decline they see in many churches. An article in *Time* magazine reported, "The central fact about mainline Protestantism in the U.S. today is that it is in deep trouble. The stunning turnabout is apparent in the unprecedented hemorrhaging of memberships in the three major faiths that date from colonial times."[2]

Those three major denominations are the United Church of Christ, down 20 percent since 1965; the Presbyterian church, down 25 percent; and the Episcopal church, down 28 percent.

One man in such a church that is conservative and close to the typical evangelical church commented about this decline. "Dissatisfaction with governance at the top levels and a weak pulpit ministry has lessened my interest in recent years."

WHAT EXACTLY IS THE PROBLEM?

So what is the problem that people are experiencing?

"The main reason I've never joined a church is simply because I knew I couldn't give it the time I should," says Carey Price, a furniture sales manager in a Sears store in Hunt Valley, Maryland. "Really giving yourself takes a lot of time," he said. " And I just don't have it with the other ministries I'm involved in."

Carey is involved heavily in working with a Christian camp and is a leader in CBMC, Christian Businessmen's Committee, a businessmen's organization that seeks to make disciples in the context of one's daily work. For personal reasons he sees these activities as opposed to service in his church as the significant use of his time.

Another businessman, Dave Buettell, a sales engineer with Reliance Electric in Baltimore told me, "Frankly, when is enough enough? You get pressure from people in the church. You feel a responsibility to your family. But mostly you just feel guilty. You feel you can't say no. It's an incredible tension."

Randy Schiller summed it all up this way: "I never used to have this problem until I became a member of a church."

MEETINGED OUT

Jesus did discipleship. The modern church generally only talks about it. Jesus had a ministry. The modern church, unfortunately, seems to be an endless stream of meetings.

Dr. Joseph Werner, a podiatrist in Cockeysville, Maryland, runs four offices and has three other partners. He's on the board of directors of two Christian schools, is heavily involved in CBMC, like Carey Price above, and also spends many of his weekends in church. He says, "Our biggest problem is the inability to have a consistent family meal at home. Too often I'm out for evening meetings and have my wife and children meet me outside the home for dinner between work and meetings. Meetings have become a four-letter word to my children. Too often I'm not able to help with homework or their projects. Nothing is done at a leisurely pace in our home with any family member. Taking a break usually requires vacation time or at least having the phone off the hook."

In some churches you can spend most of your life in meetings. Worship meetings. Committee meetings. Youth group meetings. Sunday school class meetings. Social gatherings. You name it. Fellowship is the reason, but meetings are the season.

One man, who asked to remain anonymous, said, "My dad spent a lot of time in the church. He had his own business. And either he was working late, or was at church. He hardly ever did anything with me. I resented it. I still do."

Too Much!

As you study the New Testament, you don't get the impression that there were meetings on the level and at the pace of present-day society. Most of the "meetings" you find in the book of Acts are either spontaneous evangelistic "events" or prayer times organized in response to some special event. Much of the teaching was done house by house, or in the Temple. There simply does not appear to be the systematization you find in the church today.

The Substitute

The question is, have we substituted meetings for true spirituality?

Don Hawkins, at one time connected with the Minirth-Meier Clinic and for some time the host of the radio program by the same name, comments, "The evangelical church has fed into the hurried society by scheduling too many events—and then pressuring people into doing too much. All in the name of Christian service."

He adds that the church itself is "very reluctant to jettison programs. They feel that somehow they're displeasing God—violating Scripture—if they terminate a program or two. And the false guilt factor goes up."

Bob Osburn, a missionary working with internationals in Minnesota, said, "I believe that the evangelical church is far too activity-oriented. Church will eat up your discretionary time."

Brent Brooks, a church-planting pastor in Columbia, Maryland, sees this as a serious problem and hindrance not only to real spirituality and success but to building disciples. "The multiple meeting format and the heavily bureaucratized structure of most churches," he says, "gives them trouble getting commitment from their people. People feel stressed out. Sunday used to be a day of relaxation." But now it's hurry, hurry, hurry— from one meeting to the next.

VALUE IN MEETINGS?

No one is claiming that the church ought to terminate all meetings, committee work, group ministries, socials, and other forms of fellowship, evangelism, and worship. But it's obvious that people are reaching their limits. Considering that Sunday night services and even Wednesday prayer meetings are a modern invention, there's nothing sacred in either. God has not given us the form; He's provided the function. That is, He's told us what to do; He hasn't told us in all cases, and especially in the area of meetings and services, how to do it.

QUALITY!

Perhaps part of the problem is not the meetings, but the quality of the ones we attend. In many cases they're just not up to snuff, soul, or spirit! Even though large numbers of evangelical churches are growing, there are evangelical churches that are in a holding pattern or in the same kind of decline as the main line denominations.

Unfortunately, the joy and power of Christianity —which is people living out their faith in their homes, workplaces, and marketplaces—has been subtly transformed. Now we may meet in the church to keep the machine going rather than meet in order to be trained to go out.

The end result is that people burn out or burn up. Some even rebel. What they're saying is: "Either make the meetings you have more meaningful and more worthwhile, or I won't come."

Is This Selfishness?

Is this plain sin and selfishness?

To some degree—but not only on the part of the church member. Sin runs right through the whole spectrum, from pastors and leaders who are neither pastoring nor leading, to the lazy lamb who doesn't want to lose his TV time.

There must be change. But what kind of change?

The complaints I have seen about the church and its many meetings may be summarized as follows:

> Too many services that don't teach, inspire, or induce real worship
>
> Too many meetings
>
> Confusing and poorly run meetings
>
> Meetings that fail to reach decisions and must be rescheduled
>
> Meetings that fail to reach a quorum and must be rescheduled
>
> Meetings that go on and on ad infinitum
>
> Meetings that have no content
>
> Meetings run by people who like meetings
>
> Too many other outside activities
>
> Too many activities that are more attractive than church activities
>
> Too many things I have to force my kids, my family, and myself to go to
>
> Too little real worship and enjoyment of God

After a while, a person gets so tired of it all, he pulls back and says, "What's the use? I'll do something else." So he gets involved in meaningful organizations outside the church—parachurch or otherwise.

What's the answer? Again, we'll explore that in the next two sections.

NOTES

1. Robert H. Surpless, Letter to the editor, *Moody Monthly,* July-August, 1989, p. 10.
2. Richard N. Ostling, "Those Mainline Blues," *Time,* May 22, 1988, p. 94.

3

Me: Too Much to Do,
Too Little Time to Do It In

America has run out of time.
—*Time*, cover story, April 24, 1989

[The American] is always in a hurry.
—Alexis de Tocqueville, 1840

Psychologists have found a new syndrome in the modern American. It's called the OOC syndrome. OOC, for "out of control." It's an acronym "that awaits high-achievers who burn themselves out acquiring those other initials: MBA, CPA, J.D., M.D., PC, VCR, CD, IRA."[1]

Esther Orioli, a management consultant in San Francisco, says that this condition is often accompanied by tremendous fear. "OOC's get into staying busy so they won't notice that they're scared to death. A moving target is hard to hit. If we sat still long enough, we'd notice that our work life is in chaos and our home life is a shambles."[2]

Nancy Ryan, a marriage counselor in San Jose, California, adds that the OOC ends up in a vicious circle. "We want more, and in the process we end up with less. Less quality relationships. And a less quality relationship with ourselves.

"Our self-esteem is low so we say, 'If I just had a new house, or lived in a better neighborhood, or had better clothes, I'd be happy.' It's easier to buy a new car to make you feel better than to focus inside yourself to find out who you are."[3]

What happens to the OOC is that he or she hurries faster and faster, and to where? Who knows? "Just keep moving and no one will bug you."

What ultimately happens to the OOC is total disorder, from socks on the floor, underwear under the bed, and sheets that haven't been changed in four months, to an inability to concentrate and a haggard look everywhere he goes.

RESULTS OF DISORDER

These social analysts admittedly are not coming from a biblical perspective. However, Christians have noted the same kind of trouble in their own and other lives. Instead of order, they find disorder. Instead of purpose and direction, they find a helter-skelter mess.

In *Ordering Your Private World* Gordon MacDonald has written about this kind of personal life disarray. He notices that his desk takes on a cluttered appearance. His car is a mess. He becomes paranoid that people will find out about him. He fails to keep appointments, return calls, and meet deadlines. He invests his time in unproductive tasks. He doesn't feel optimistic or interested in his work. Intimacy with God evaporates. Personal relationships become shallow and unaffirming. He ends up not liking himself, his job, or anything else in his world.[4]

Such a person is out of control. He's lost touch with himself, his world, and his Lord. It's a sloppy way to live. Worse than that, though, disorder of this magnitude breeds discouragement, disillusionment, and ultimately despair.

THE OUT-OF-CONTROL CHRISTIAN

The out-of-control Christian—the one in such a hurry to get anywhere but where he is—finds that several things begin happening in his life. In his book *Little House on the Freeway* Tim Kimmel catalogs seven symptoms of the hurried and out-of-control life-style.[5]

"You can't relax." Got to do something. Now. And it better get big results. Now!

Brent Brooks told me, "Too often in the church we teach the idea that activity equals spirituality. We tell people to get into Bible study, pray, witness, use your gifts, spend time with your family, serve in the church, do a good job at work. We load them down with a tremendous burden of guilt. Young parents get stressed out because of the kids' schedule. Running here, running there. I think what's needed is to teach people to limit themselves in each area, to strive for balance. You simply can't have it all!"

This kind of anxiety often finds its roots in an improper fear of God. In *Discipleship Journal* Kevin Miller has called attention to an observation made by Robert Hudnut, a Presbyterian pastor and the author of *This People, This Parish.* Hudnut, Miller says, "points out that there are really only two motivating forces in our lives: love and fear.

"Both are valid, but love is the sweeter and the stronger of the two. So I've learned to ask myself this question: 'Am I doing this more out of love (for God) or fear (that He won't love me if I don't)?' I'd like to reach the point where every quiet time, every Bible study, every journal entry is done because I love God so much for saving me. Less and less do I want to do these things because I'm afraid He won't love me quite as much if I don't."[6]

The fear Miller refers to leads to the inability ever to relax. You just aren't doing enough. No matter how good, how spiritual, how committed you are, it's not enough for God, the church, or you.

"You can't enjoy quiet." Got to have that noise. Jump in the car, switch on the radio while you stomp on the gas. The moment you walk in the door, turn on the

stereo or the TV. What's "quiet"? Who knows? "Neva
hoid uh da bum!" It's a foreign country you never want
to visit, something akin to those places in darkest Africa
where the only noise you hear is the lion roaring in the
night or the water buffalo stomping down the road.

Jeri Sweany, a homemaker, working mother, and
struggling writer in Annapolis, Maryland, told me,
"How often are we still? I saw this Bible verse—'Be still
and know that I am God'—next to a family's entrance
and the person told me she'd put it there to remind everyone in the family to slow down and think about what
God was saying or wanting them to do. We can't really
know God until we are still. I haven't conquered the
rush-rush syndrome, but I'm seeking to have a more
subdued life-style so that I can concentrate on the
things that are important."

That stillness is something that eludes many of us.
We can't stop long enough to find out if the quiet quiets
our soul.

"You never feel satisfied with what you have." No
matter what you've got, how much you've done, where
you've been, *it's not enough!* Thus, a big reason for our
time crunch is our expenditures. If we extend ourselves
financially, we'll have to invest the time to make up the
money.

It's such a simple principle, yet we often overlook
it. Eileen Merrell told me, "The basic principle I learned
was that my time crunch was because I was doing it all.
Now, nothing is committed without our constant response, 'Let us pray about it overnight.'"

She added, "We constantly evaluate where our
time is spent. If it is in extra part-time jobs, then we
evaluate where our money is going. Mike [her husband]
and I look at it this way: If we need to pay for it, we need
to pray for it! Many times the extra item just isn't
needed."

But that's a hard outlook to establish in this day
and age of "got to have it now."

"You can't get anything finished." That project is still sitting on the shelf—after two years. That hobby you've been meaning to start never quite finds its way onto your "to do some relaxation and fun" list. That night out your wife has pled for never seems convenient. "I have a project to finish up, honey."

Paul J. Meyer said, "Experience proves that most time is wasted, not in hours, but in minutes. A bucket with a small hole in the bottom gets just as empty as a bucket that is deliberately kicked over."

Bill Meyer [not related], a management consultant, recently studied a hard-driving, eighty-hour-a-week investment banker on Wall Street to help him better use his time. Meyer most remembers the man's two briefcases. "They were the fattest, most imposing briefcases I'd ever seen."

The results of his study? "After three days, Meyer and his client sat down and replayed the hundreds of activities recorded in Meyer's notebook. Eighty percent of them—that 80 percent of everything the investment banker did over three days—turned out to be busy work that ultimately did nothing to increase the man's productivity. Meyer's log overflowed with notes of unnecessary meetings, redundant phone conversations, and even the few minutes wasted each day in packing and unpacking those bulging briefcases. As Meyer's log suggests, the correct question isn't, 'How long do I work?' but, 'How effectively do I work?'"[7]

The inability to get anything finished infects everything, from the smallest household chore to the year-long project at work. Time not only runs out, it runs you down till you're ready to collapse in the dust.

"You need constant approval and feel overworked." "Tell me how I'm doing, please, and don't be critical about it!" For some reason, the harried person is often a "people pleaser" who needs steady injections of encouragement to keep going. But that's to be understood. Who would want to maintain his schedule without

someone breathing down his neck, "You're wonderful! I love you! Keep going! You can make it!" But the problem with such encouragement is that often beneath it all runs this undercurrent: "And if you don't satisfy my demands, I'll break your back!"

Mary Ann Dean, a retired schoolteacher now living in Arizona, put it this way: "I was caught in the time crunch for years. But through a book I read, I began to see how I had learned to work and volunteer to gain acceptance. It showed me how I felt compelled to work to please others. I also saw how I needed to control others and be a people pleaser. All of it sapped time and energy."

How did she escape? "I was ill for three years and am still not my old self, but with much improvement. During this time, by reading many books and rethinking my life I have come to feel the time crunch is more than too few hours in the day. It was for me a part of my personality and way of life. As I began to learn why I had to be involved and so busy, I began to change my goals and behavior. I now find it much easier to evaluate all areas of my life before saying yes."

Sometimes God has to put you flat on your back before you'll take the time to be still and hear Him!

Jeri Sweany commented on the same issue: "A Scripture that has often hit home with me is Galatians 1:10. 'Am I now trying to win the approval of men, or of God? Or am I trying to please men?' I frequently find myself being a people-pleaser. And being a people-pleaser often leads to doing things I really don't have time for. This verse, when I meditate on it, helps me focus on what I am doing and why I am doing it. We can be very busy helping people when that may be what God wants us to do at that particular time. Maybe He just wants us to be quiet and spend time with Him."

"Underneath the calm, you're ready to explode." The family secret is driving you crazy and at any moment it

may get out, so you guard yourself carefully. You feel so hemmed in and frustrated, you literally want to scream. The fuse is lit, the flame burns towards its mark. But you frantically pull on the line trying to stretch it farther so that it doesn't explode.

In his little book *Power Through Prayer*, E. M. Bounds quotes William Wilberforce: "This perpetual hurry of business and company ruins me in soul if not in body. More solitude and earlier hours! I suspect I have been allotting habitually too little time to religious exercises, as private devotions and religious meditation, Scripture-reading, etc. Hence I am lean and cold and hard."

Lean. Cold. Hard. That's the heart of the person caught in the hurry-scurry syndrome. He or she becomes a robot, all the emotion pushed out. Nonetheless, it all boils somewhere down below like volcanic lava, building pressure and temperature to the eruption point.

C. S. Lewis zeroed in on the cause when he wrote in *The Screwtape Letters*, "There is nothing like suspense and anxiety for barricading a human's mind against the Enemy. He wants men to be concerned with what they do; our business is to keep them thinking about what will happen to them."

The devil loves Christians "ready to explode." All he needs then is the right button, the right torch.

"You've got to win—at any price. You can't be happy unless you're successful." The Super Mom, Super Dad, and Super Kids are stepping all over one another to make it.

As a member of the sixties generation I grew up with a strong belief in having it all. "You can have it all," someone told us. I don't remember who he was, where he articulated it, and why he gripped us so. But I'd like to confront him some day and say, "Liar, liar, pants on fire!"

In truth, you can't have it all. In fact, you can't have much of that "all." Hurry won't get it for you. Neither will racing around, dropping out, giving in, or going berserk.

TIME-KILLERS AND TIME-FILLERS

If the OOC syndrome, the picture of the disorganized person, and the hurried life-style are all the symptoms, then what are the problems for the Christian in his day-by-day life?

> Too many desirable activities beckoning for your attention
>
> Too many important choices to make every day
>
> Too much information coming at you
>
> Too many voices calling for your attention
>
> Too many things you want and can have, at the plink of a credit card
>
> Too many people telling you what's important
>
> Too many entertaining entertainments
>
> Too many things that we "need" to function well
>
> Too many tempting temptations
>
> Too much guilt

On top of it all, we just don't know what counts anymore. Life becomes a hundred-yard dash through a fog. Not only don't you know where the finish line is, you don't even know if you're in the right race, or if there is a race, or if the race is worth racing in.

But there are solutions. People of yesteryear . . .

> didn't live as long,
>
> had few modern conveniences,
>
> had a shorter workday because of their lack of lighting,
>
> took much longer to do the simple jobs like washing and cooking,

. . . and yet, in many cases, they still produced quality products, wrote worthwhile books, and cast long shadows upon succeeding generations.

And we have the same Bible they did.

NOTES

1. Claudia Morain, "The Stress of Having It All," *Washington Post*, September 22, 1988, p. C5.
2. Ibid.
3. Ibid.
4. Gordon MacDonald, *Ordering Your Private World* (Nashville, Tenn.: Thomas Nelson, 1984), pp. 71-72.
5. Tim Kimmel, *Little House on the Freeway* (Portland, Oreg.: Multnomah, 1987), pp. 17-28.
6. Kevin A. Miller, "I Don't Feel Like a Very Good Christian," *Discipleship Journal*, no. 47 (1988), p. 9.
7. Ford S. Worthy, "You're Probably Working Too Hard," *Fortune*, April 27, 1987, p. 133.

4

The Family: Hurry Sweet Hurry

Nobody eats together anymore because we all have differing schedules.

—Woody Price

Michael Green put it this way: "The battle for the Christian family is over. The family lost. The home has become a stopping place to store goods and have a meal—occasionally."

Everyone admits the family's in trouble. Crime, drugs, divorce, alcohol—all are wreaking the usual havoc. But what about the problem with time?

Cathy Trost observed in the *Wall Street Journal* that "with women working outside the home in record numbers, men are feeling increased pressure to spend more time with their children and to help around the house. Employers, however, generally haven't made it easy for them to do so. The result is that today's working fathers are feeling the anxieties that have plagued working mothers for years. 'Stress,' says Bradley Googins, an associate professor at the Boston University School of Social Work, 'is becoming more equitable.'"[1]

Time magazine reported, "No one quite bargained for the Middle-Class Squeeze, what Paula Rayman, a sociologist at Wellesley College's Stone Center, calls 'falling behind while getting ahead.' The prices of houses have soared, inflation erodes paychecks, wages are stagnant, and medical and tuition costs continue to skyrocket. So now it takes two paychecks to fund what many imagined was a middle class life. 'The American Dream is very much intact,' says Rayman. 'It's just more expensive.'"[2]

Having both Mom and Dad work makes it even tougher. Fifty-seven percent of U.S. families are in that situation. But "someone still has to find the time to make lunches and pediatrician appointments, shop, cook, fix the washer, do the laundry, take the children to choir practice. Single-parent households are squeezed even more."[3]

THOSE SINGLE PARENTS

Speaking of single parent households, just how is that situation holding up? The 1986 Census Bureau reported that 8.8 million mothers are living without their children's fathers. Of that number, only 24 percent actually receive all the child support they were granted in court.[4] That adds to the squeeze on everyone.

CONSTANT CHANGES

Parents today speak of a "balancing act" that is akin to Tevye's fiddler in the play "Fiddler on the Roof."

Lois Ednie, a Christian homemaker in Hershey, Pennsylvania, comments on the effect having children has on a marriage and a couple's use of time: "Having children caused us to have more responsibilities away from each other. We (my husband and I) no longer ate lunch together at work. We were no longer involved in youth ministry together. We find it a constant balancing act between family and home responsibilities and Doug's job, pro-life work, school involvement, and Bible study."

MORE RELATIONSHIPS

This balancing act is especially critical when you consider the number of relationships that are going on in a crowded home. When a young wife and husband decide to have children the number of interpersonal relationships increases exponentially.

Susan Osburn, a wife and mother whose husband, Bob, works as a missionary in Minnesota, said, "The number of relationships between people living in a home doesn't add when another person comes into it; it multiplies. For instance when Bob and I married, there was only one relationship. Then when our first son was born, there were not three relationships, but four:

Bob and I
Robby and I
Bob and Robby and I
Bob and Robby

"Then when Joey came along there were more. It multiplies like this. With two children, you have four people. The number of relationships is 4 times 3 times 2 times 1, which equals 24. We have four children. That's 6 times 5 times 4 times 3 times 2 times 1, or, in effect, 720 different relationships going on!"

The result? Susan says, "I discovered I wasn't (and will never be) a 'supermom.' I have had to make changes in my own life, my marriage, and my parenting in order to survive in an emotionally healthy way."

Tim Kimmel agrees. "It's funny how easily we can find ourselves in a fast-forward mind-set. It doesn't require a conscious effort. Actually, it's the logical outcome of the forces surrounding us each day.

"I see it in my own family. The Kimmels have found that being hurried comes naturally—while being at rest requires an ongoing appraisal of priorities. All of us who are serious about our spiritual life and our family life must counter the forces threatening our ability to maintain rest."[5]

SOLVING THE PROBLEM

How, then, do many parents solve the problem of too many mouths calling for their mommer or their popper? Day care. Babysitters. A nanny.

I've noticed that when I'm at home with my daughters I often rent them a movie or two to watch while I write. The movie—"The Land Before Time," or "Captain January," or "Cinderella"—becomes a surrogate dad or mom. When my daughter came downstairs one day and said, "Daddy, I'm so tired of movies," I knew I'd made a mistake. I asked her what she liked most about when we're together. She said, "When we play a game, or you read me a story." When I tried to remember how often I'd done such things with her, I was stunned and guilt-ridden. Here I was missing the most important formative years of her life and giving them over to a television.

EVEN MORE PERSONAL

Some of the bad effects, though, are even more intense. Eileen Merrell, quoted earlier, struggled with the time crunch in her home for a long time. "It used to have a bad effect on all of us—bickering, not listening to the kids, spending too much money on fast food and then fighting over money—having clothes dirty that you want to wear—going to church and not listening to the sermon because our worries were so loud in our heads."

Dr. Joseph Werner reported, "I have professional, family, and vocational (ministry) work which all demand time in excess of what I can possibly provide. The problem is not in the time I do give to each area, but in the need to give more time to each area. That need is unfortunately determined by others who never seem satisfied with the time I do give."

It's almost like the mother bird who comes home with the worm, only to find five demanding beaks wide open and screaming, "Give it to me! Give it to me!"

Doug White, a UPS delivery man, added, "The last four years of my employment has caused me to be at home in a freetime setting for about one hour per day during the week. This has caused my patience level to be short on the occasions when I must wait in line, or am stuck in traffic. I am a new father, and my son needs daily interaction with me as well as I with him. I see any delay as a direct obstacle to our time together."

That tension brings anger and frustration into the home. Even though one may be committed to Christian principles and the bearing of the fruit of the Spirit (patience, kindness, gentleness), irritations can take over. The time crunch can make you look and feel like the resident ogre.

Woody Price, a computer whiz and recent college graduate, commented, "Nobody eats together anymore because we all have differing schedules."

Dinner in my own family's home growing up was prime conversation and fellowship time. No more. The members of the household are like ships passing each other on the sea in the night.

THE PRESSURES

What then are the primary pressures that the family is facing?

Pressure from our culture: *"You can have it all—if you'll give it all you got."* The world makes us believe we can have it all, then it finds ways to make it happen— even if that puts us under a pile of guilt, financial worries, and fear. With automated bank tellers, we can get our money at the push of the button. Through the junk mail credit marketers, we can get "instant credit" for that dream house, dream trip, or dream machine at the sign of a pen. Fastfood serves our burgers up fast and hot. We can even eat them in our car hurtling down the road at sixty miles per hour toward our next critical destination.

Pressure in our workplace: *"If you want to stay ahead, you'll have to run."* That means fifty, sixty, seventy hours on the job. Don't eat lunch, do some sit-ups. Give your kids "quality time" and "don't worry, be happy." Take the wife out to eat on Saturday night. Even if you have to clinch a business deal then, they can always reach you on your cellular belt phone.

Pressure from the media: *"Keep the Indians restless."* Keep telling them through commercials and entertainment what they ought to want, then help them get it—even if what you're selling has no value once it's bought. The name of the game in advertising is to hold out the carrot, then get them to third-mortgage the farm in order to get it.

Pressure in the church: *"We have something for everyone every night of the week."* Programs multiply. The family gets stretched. Everyone's going every which way, except together.

Pressure within the self: *"I want it NOW."* The epitome of sin is an unwillingness to wait on God for His good gifts. Instead we want it now. Those who wait are supposedly the fools. Life is passing you by.

As Tim Kimmel says, the hurried life-style is something "our culture values, business rewards, the media exploits, and our egos demand."[6]

NOTES

1. Cathy Trost, "Men, Too, Wrestle with Career-Family Stress," *Wall Street Journal*, November 1, 1988, p. B1.
2. Nancy Gibbs, "How America Has Run Out of Time," *Time*, April 24, 1989, p. 60.
3. Ibid.
4. "Child Support Often Proves Elusive," *Wall Street Journal*, May 2, 1989, p. B1.
5. Tim Kimmel, *Little House on the Freeway* (Multnomah, Oreg.: Multnomah, 1987), p. 21.
6. Ibid., pp. 29-33.

5

Work:
40 Hours Just Doesn't Cut It!

I flew 80,000 miles last year. You start losing touch with things. My work is research, which at its best is contemplative. If you get into this mode of running around, you don't have time to reflect.
—A management consultant, quoted in *Time* magazine

Carol Hymowitz interviewed for the *Wall Street Journal* a number of people who have opted for a simpler, less fast-paced life-style. One of the persons she interviewed cast the truth of the career/work situation in its starkest light. His name is Tom Kosnik, until recently a professor at Harvard Business School. He said, "I have real doubts that anyone can sustain 70-hour workweeks for very long."[1]

Fantastic! This man is speaking to our times.

But what else does he say? " . . . but doing just 40 hours in a demanding job, especially where you're facing global competition, isn't enough."

A sales vice president at a consumer products company agrees: "Time is money, and if you aren't putting that time in, you won't be considered for the top spots."[2]

As a result, many Christians find themselves in a terrifying and mystifying dilemma—getting ahead in their careers without compromising the Christian principles they've long believed and practiced.

WORKING MOMS

In the work world of today, there are a number of obvious problems when it comes to the time crunch people feel. One of the first is working mothers. Studies reveal, as I quoted earlier, that more than 60 percent of mothers with children under eighteen work. With that statistic comes all the trappings of the harried, worried parent. Latchkey children. High child care costs. Precious little time for the little ones.

What is not seen, though, is the fact that this lifestyle carries a high pressure tag for the working mother. Many women end up working a literal "second shift" when they get home. A new book, *The Second Shift: Working Parents and the Revolution at Home,* by sociologist Arlie Hochschild, points out the problem in deft and startling detail.

Hochschild writes, "Most women work one shift at the office or factory and a 'second shift' at home."[3] That adds up to over 15 extra hours a week for such women.

Another researcher, John P. Robinson, of the University of Maryland, involved some 5,000 men and women in a 1985 study. He found that women with children under five average 22.5 hours of housework a week. Those with children over five average 19.9 hours. What about their husbands? Cut the numbers in half. What we're talking about is time. Women in the work force not only have less time for the important things in life, they have much less than they might think.

In contrast, consider the curmudgeonly professor of law in the television program "The Paper Chase" who always left work at 5:00 P.M. Why? Because, as he told his students, there were other important things for him to do besides just his job. That from a secular, Christ-rejecting television program.

THE BROKEN HOME

Still, the figures get even worse in the case of broken homes. Single parent homes have increased dramatically in the last decade. The Census Bureau recently reported that 54 percent of black children live with one parent. Over 15.3 million children of all races live in single parent homes today. And "1.9 million others live with neither parent."[4] The reasons are obvious: divorce, or the fact that the mother was never married to begin with.

What is even more tragic is the fact that so few of the missing fathers have lived up to their financial obligations. In 1986 the Census Bureau discovered that some 8.8 million mothers live without their children's fathers. When they took their pleas to court, only 61 percent were even granted some form of alimony. But only 24 percent actually receive what they were awarded.

This kind of financial burden wreaks havoc in the area of time for everyone. It means more hours spent trying to make ends meet for those single moms. Also, more time helping people, counseling them, and tracking them through the courts. For the church and its members, it also increases the burden, because divorce is affecting Christians too.

GLOBAL COMPETITION

Many Christians will not find themselves in the single parent problem. But all will face the effects of the new international economy in which companies struggle against competition on a global scale. Fewer big companies can survive today without battling for a niche in the economies of Europe, Japan, Africa, South America, and even Communist nations. With the emerging freedom in Eastern Europe, and possibly Russia and China, there will be even stiffer competition for those markets.

For the average worker that means more hours spent in sales, product development, marketing, and every other level of effort.

An engineer with an international division of Mitsubishi working in corrugating machinery told me, "Business travel is the primary thief of my home time." He wishes he could lead a Scout troop or coach kids' sports. But right now with his work situation, too much travel is required. He can be gone on the average of one to three days a week, as well as one and two weeks at a crack.

Time magazine quoted one management consultant as saying, "I flew 80,000 miles last year. You start losing touch with things. My work is research, which at its best is contemplative. If you get into this mode of running around, you don't have time to reflect."[5]

This global economy means it takes more hours and effort just to stay alive in business. Christians and everyone else must "stay on their toes" and "move fast," or they'll soon find themselves not only left behind the pack, but packing for another job!

TECHNOLOGY

Another of the strange dichotomies that has occurred in the workplace are the so-called time-saving devices that have been invented in recent years. Testimony before a Senate subcommittee in 1967 prophesied that by 1985 Americans would be working only twenty-two hours a week. People could retire at the age of thirty-eight! Amazing things like the personal computer, lap-top computer, microwave oven, VCR, and other computerized systems for the home and auto would streamline everything. We'd have nothing but leisure, pleasure, and treasure.

Not so. Instead we have fifty- to seventy-hour work-weeks with no end in sight. "Technology is increasing the heartbeat," says James Trunzo, a Manhattan architect. "We are inundated with information. The mind can't handle it all. The pace is so fast now, I sometimes feel like a gunfighter dodging bullets."[6]

In my own office if someone wants to contact me from Japan they can call me on the phone, write me on the telex, or send me an image of it on the telefax. If that doesn't work, my "sky pager" will surely beep me wherever I may try to hide. If I can't make the mail deadline, my editor just says, "Send it by Federal Express. Or better yet, hook up the computer modem and send us the article by electronic mail."

Good grief! Where to find a place to sit down that doesn't have noise!

THE SIMPLE FACTS ABOUT MONEY

Why do we work? To get money. For what? To live.

But living today is very expensive. Making the money takes time. And to make more of it takes more time. Eileen Merrell told me, "At one time both my husband and I were laid off, and it has taken years to get over it financially. Even though my husband found work in a few months, we'd bought so much on credit, it almost ruined us—financially and emotionally."

Where does all the money go? Again, the ubiquitous Census Bureau knows. In 1987, the average American household spent $24,414. For what? The highest amount, $7,569, went for housing expenses. After that was $4,600 for auto expenses. Food chewed up another $3,664. Another $2,175 went for personal insurance and pensions. Clothing carried away $1,446. We were entertained to the tune of $1,193, and our doctors, hospitals, and other forms of health care took $1,135.[7]

But all of this is quite meaningless unless you compare it to the spending capabilities of a generation ago. Richard Reeves wrote in an editorial in the *Baltimore Sun* titled "Generations Ago," "It's tougher being young today. All the money and glamour and new entertainments around these days give kids more choices.

"Two . . . economic realities have changed since I grew up. My generation could take charge of our lives very early because: (1) You could work your way through college; (2) You could buy a home. My college tuition was $800 a year, and, even in 1960 I could earn quite a bit more than that doing summer and part-time work. My kids can't earn $8,737 a year, the average private college tuition these days. The down payment on the first house I bought, in 1965, was $6,000—not an impossible sum, especially with some help from parents.

"They don't build them that way anymore. For many kids, including some of mine, the best way to get a house is going to be waiting for the old folks to pass on. But we all live longer now, and the old folks don't feel or act that old anymore."[8]

For your information, the so-called good life takes one household and two paychecks, according to that incredible, omnipresent Census Bureau. They recently revealed that a family needs combined earnings of $56,605 to provide for all basic costs and have enough left over for some of the luxuries.[9]

Such figures are just about enough to give most of us under forty a faster heartbeat on the way to the grindstone.

THE FUTURE

If you've read this far and you're tempted to say, "It has got to get better in the future," perhaps you ought to think again. Several "looking ahead" articles I found reported these realities for our tomorrow:

You'll be faxing your lunch order to the deli from your kitchen—but you'll have to pay more for the delivery.

Your "compu-robot" will check the refridge and make any orders to the supermarket by computer—but the supermarket will automatically deduct your payment from your bank account.

Your family will more than likely "graze" when they eat fewer family meals—but take heart, they'll also be able to "beep" you when they really need you!

You may work in your home—but your boss will be only a "belt-phone" call away.

You may get much more done in the average day—but you'll still only have twenty-four hours in which to do it.

One article closed with these words, after chronicling the daily routine of a high level manager named Peter Smith, who works for a home-appliance company: "6:00 P.M. Before heading to the airport, Mr. Smith uses his video phone to give his daughters a good-night kiss and to talk about the next day's schedule with his wife. Learning that she must take an unexpected trip herself the next evening, he promises to catch the SuperConcorde home in time to put the kids to sleep himself."[10]

IF THAT DOESN'T . . .

. . . clang your chimes, I used to think Sunday was the day of rest. But today, I got several unexpected phone calls. Two from veterans' organizations asking for donations, one from a woman asking to talk to my wife about home day care, and a fourth from the local city newspaper—which I canceled over a month ago—asking if I was satisfied with their service!

THE BOMBSHELL

So there's the problem in a bombshell. In the last five chapters, we've looked at five areas that must be addressed—God, the church, the self, the family, and work. These issues pertain to us whether we're married or single, divorced or widowed, working, in school, or retired. Our answers to them will influence how we work, how we play, and how we worship.

Still, perhaps at this point you're thinking in altogether terms—something like, "Maranatha—even so, come Lord Jesus"!

And for more reasons than one!

I hope then you're ready to move on. The rest of this book will help you find a way not only to cope, but to find true hope.

NOTES

1. Carol Hymowitz, "Stepping Off the Fast Track," *Wall Street Journal*, June 13, 1989, p. B1.

2. Ibid.

3. Mary Maushard, "On the Second Shift, Women Still Suffer with the Workload," *Baltimore Sun*, September 4, 1989, p. 1B.

4. Spencer Rich, "Single-Parent Families Increase," *Washington Post*, February 16, 1988, p. A7.

5. Nancy Gibbs, "How America Has Run Out of Time," *Time*, April 24, 1989, p. 60.

6. Ibid.

7. "Household Spending: Where Do Dollars Go?" *Wall Street Journal*, August 21, 1989, p. B1.

8. Richard Reeves, "Generations Ago," *Baltimore Sun*, September 4, 1989, p. 7A.

9. Spencer Rich, "Prescription for the Good Life: 1 Household, 2 Paychecks," *Washington Post*, May 25, 2989, p. A9.

10. Carol Hymowitz, "Day in the Life of Tomorrow's Manager," *Wall Street Journal*, March 20, 1989, p. B1.

Part 2

Answers:
The Divine Line on Time

6

Choose This Day
Whom You Will Serve

If Jesus Christ be God and died for me, then no sacrifice for Him can be too great.

—C. T. Studd

Whom will you serve—

God or mammon (the money-driven life-style)?
the Son or self (the me-me-me life-style)?
scriptural directives or secular opinions?
the Way or the world?
the Lord or . . . (fill in the blank)?

Joshua drew the dividing line long ago in the book that goes by his name. He had reached the end of his journey. He knew he was soon to die. But he wanted to leave his people with one final exhortation and challenge.

No, it was more than a challenge. He decided to set before them the ultimate choice all of us make sometime in this life: the choice to follow, or not to follow, God in Jesus Christ. However He comes to us, He comes to each, asking, "Will you follow Me?" Our decision impacts every moment of the rest of our lives. How we use or abuse our allotment of time on earth will be determined by that choice.

Joshua said it this way: "But if serving the Lord seems undesirable to you, then choose for yourselves this day whom you will serve, whether the gods your forefathers served beyond the River, or the gods of the Amorites, in whose land you are living. But as for me and my household, we will serve the Lord" (Joshua 24:15).

Joshua drew a stark, fine, and final line. "Choose . . . whom you will serve." In other words, by whose wisdom will you make the decisions of your life—God's or the world's? Whose kingdom will you seek to build—God's or yours? Whose glory will you exalt—God's or another's? Whom will you worship—God or your own flesh?

All through history people have faced the same choice. It's a narrow way. But time is a narrow reality. We only have the now in which to do our work. Romans 13:12 says, "The night is nearly over; the day is almost here. So let us put aside the deeds of darkness and put on the armor of light."

It is late. The time is short. We can only do so much. But what we do in our now will affect our forever.

THE COMMITTED CHRISTIAN

In all probability, you are a conservative Christian. You may have known Christ for many years, or perhaps only a few. But somewhere along the line, you made a decision to follow Jesus.

I salute you for that and want to encourage you in your commitment: Press on. (Without being in a hurry to get there!)

Just the same, perhaps you need to reassert that commitment in the matter of how you use your time. Or perhaps you've never made such a commitment.

Either way, this chapter is for you.

COUNTING THE COST

This is not a decision without great hope and glory.

Robert Laidlaw, at eighteen in New Zealand, decided to give a 10 percent tithe of his income to the Lord. He wrote in his diary at age twenty, "Before money gets a grip on my heart, by the grace of God I enter into the following pledge with the Lord that: I will give 10 percent of all I earn up to _____.

"If the Lord blesses me with _____, I will give 15 percent of all I earn.

"If the Lord blesses me with _____, I will give 20 percent of all I earn.

"If the Lord blesses me with _____, I will give 25 percent of all I earn.

"The Lord help me to keep this promise for the sake of Christ who gave all for me."

When Laidlaw reached twenty-five, he wrote, "I have decided to change the graduated scale and start now giving half (50 percent) of all my earnings."

Laidlaw chose each day to serve the Lord, not other gods—money, hurry, pleasure, or anything else. He ended up at seventy as one of the most successful businessmen in New Zealand. He wrote, "I want to bear testimony that, in spiritual communion and in material things, God has blessed me one hundredfold, and has graciously entrusted to me a stewardship far beyond my expectations when, as a lad of 18, I started to give God a definite portion of my wages."

C. T. Studd (1862-1931), a master cricket player at Eton, became one of the "Cambridge Seven" who dedicated his life to missions in the early 1880s. He gave away an inherited fortune and sailed for China with Hudson Taylor's China Inland Mission in 1885. Later, as an invalid, he began the Student Volunteer Movement (which was the precursor of Inter-Varsity, Campus Crusade for Christ, Campus Life, Youth For Christ, and other student organizations) in the 1890s. He went to India and became a pastor from 1900-1906 in the Union Church in Ootacumund, South India. After that he preached in England for some years. Finally, against his doctor's advice, he went to Africa, founding the Heart of Africa Mission in 1912. It became the present-day Worldwide Evangelization Crusade. He died in Central Africa in 1931.[2]

What motivated C. T. Studd? He wrote, "If Jesus Christ be God and died for me, then no sacrifice for Him can be too great."

The same choice that fell to Robert Laidlaw and C. T. Studd falls to each of us. Taming the time crunch is more than a matter of good principles, sound wisdom, personal discipline, and some time tips; it requires supernatural power and intervention. None of us can win the personal time Armageddon without Jesus' personal help.

HOLD NOTHING BACK

Such commitment is not easy for many of us. But if you're serious about gaining new charge over your life, you cannot do better than to commit it all "to the Lord."

What is it that people serve today? There are only three other lords besides Him who is Lord of all: the world, the flesh, and the devil. Each can take many forms. The world's ideas, principles, leaders, matinee idols, and rock stars can be our idols. When we live for rising in the corporation we are just as idolatrous as the person who lives for money, popularity, or winning the lottery.

If the world doesn't skewer us, the flesh will. Sensuality, pleasure, pride, and lust all rage within us leading us to love such things as sex, food, sleep, entertainments, music, and creature comforts.

If somehow we discipline ourselves to overcome the flesh and the world, then the devil stands in the wings ever willing to add us to his collection of worshipers. Every form of religion (except Christ's) is his ploy to derail people into the ditch of hell. Every temptation to go our way (or the devil's) over God's, is an attempt to bag us permanently.

All these life-styles affect how we use time. Without commitment to the Bible and to the One who created time, we are lost in an amusement park of unending, worthless diversions.

I once heard a pastor speak of how he was invited to a philosophy class to speak on the subject of the Christian view of sex. He knew he had to plan his strategy well. So when he stood before the group of students, he told them, "What I am going to tell you today will run converse to everything you believe and desire. You will not accept it, you will not want it, and you will scorn it."

One student raised his hand and asked why. The pastor said, "Because you have not committed yourself to a biblical view of life. And you do not know and love the Lord Jesus Christ. Only with those two things would you be willing even to consider my words."

The same student then said, "Then maybe you need to tell us how to know and love Jesus Christ."

That gave that pastor the perfect opportunity to give that class the gospel message.

Thus, I have to say right now that this book will make no sense to you if you are not committed to the Scripture and the Lord of the Scripture. You will scoff at it. You will reject it. And you will call it foolishness.

But I can also assure you that if you come from the standpoint of affirming Christ's life, death for human sin, personal deity, and everlasting lordship, you will find in these pages new hope and direction. He can lead you far beyond the pages written here.

THE COMMITMENT

What is the commitment required?

A Haitian pastor illustrated it in this way. A man decided to sell his house for $2,000. A poor man wanted to buy it but couldn't afford the full price. The two bargained, and ultimately an agreement was reached to sell the house for $1,000, with one rule: the original owner retained ownership of one small nail that protruded over the front door.

All went well for some time, but then the original owner wanted to buy the house back. The new owner wouldn't sell. That was when that nail suddenly became important. The disgruntled former owner found a dead dog and hung it from that nail, which he still owned. Soon the house became so unlivable that the new owner was forced to sell.

Commitment to Christ is all-out. Not even a nail can be left for sin to hang its dead carcass on. If we come to him with a few nails still driven in, Satan will certainly find something to hang on them. He'll fill up our time with his reeking pleasures and diversions, and we'll soon be at the center of a life that is time-crunched, broken, and useless to God.

Still, real commitment to Christ is worked out day by day, not all at once. No one anywhere can claim to have given "all" over to Christ in a lifelong sense. Day by day he will confront new situations and problems that will require his submission all over again. Setbacks, sin, and mistakes will also drive him back to his original beliefs. It's even possible, for a time, to get off the track, to stray into sin, and get all tangled up with the world. But there is forgiveness with the Lord. He starts us over again every day. His promise is that He "who began a good work in you will carry it on to completion until the day of Christ Jesus" (Philippians 1:6).

I have found that every day is new and different. Each requires faith. Overcoming by Christ's power is not static. You don't overcome one day and sail free for the rest of your days. No, every day is a new struggle, bringing with it new battles.

That is why the life of faith is a "walk." It's step by step. But it's also a walk with Him. He will lead each of us to glory. The important thing is the outlook, the attitude that says, "I want to follow You. Lead on, gentle Savior."

AN ATTITUDE TO AVOID

Wilbur Rees illustrates the attitude we're to avoid: "I would like to buy $3 worth of God, please, not enough to explode my soul or disturb my sleep but just enough to equal a cup of warm milk or a snooze in the sunshine. I don't want enough of Him to make me love a black man or pick beets with a migrant. I want ecstasy, not transformation; I want the warmth of the womb, not a new birth. I want a pound of the Eternal in a paper sack. I would like to buy $3 worth of God, please."[3]

But God doesn't want to sell us three dollars worth of Himself. He wants to give us *all* of Himself—for free, for now, forever. All we need do is accept His leadership and love through faith in Christ, and then begin to follow Him day by day in obedience.[4]

Such obedience is not an easy thing. We often think that God wants love more than obedience. In some ways, that's true. But the obedience is the boiled down essence of love.

J. Grant Howard offers a potent thought in this regard: "Love is knowing what He expects us to do, and doing it.

"Things are quite similar in the human family. Audrey and I have four children. They love us, and through the years they have each expressed their love in a variety of ways—handmade birthday cards, a bouquet of flowers, a picture, a gift, or just spontaneous, unsolicited words of love and appreciation. But I'll tell you something that gives us even more satisfaction: when they do what we tell them to do! And believe me, it puts a lot of static in the system when they say they love us and they don't obey us. We want both affection and obedience from our kids, but if for some reason we were forced to choose between the two, we would opt for obedience. In the final analysis, cold obedience is to be preferred over warm rebellion. As a heavenly Father, God also wants both affection and obedience from His children. But He will not allow us to substitute nebulous sentiment for informed obedience."[4]

Don't confuse some "fuzzy feelings" for the real thing. Real love leads to obedience, and obedience stokes real love. That kind of love and obedience will influence every area of your time crunch.

How?

How to make that kind of commitment? It's the truth of Romans 12:1-2. "Therefore, I urge you, brothers, in view of God's mercy, to offer your bodies as living sacrifices, holy and pleasing to God—this is your spiritual act of worship. Do not conform any longer to the pattern of this world, but be transformed by the renewing of your mind. Then you will be able to test and approve what God's will is—His good, pleasing and perfect will."

Offer your body now as that living sacrifice. God will begin filling your life with the wisdom and power to control your time as He wills, not as the world, the flesh, or the devil will.

I challenge you today. Don't think you can recapture your time and life without the power of the Spirit. Multitudes of books have been written on managing our time. If the answer were as simple as a list of rules, principles, time tips, or formulas for success, then not one of us would have a problem.

But God has made us His dependents. That dependency means a daily trusting, relying, and leaning on Him. He doesn't want us to be orphans in His house, but sons and daughters. He longs to act as father, adviser, captain, and friend. As we go to Him for His counsel and direction, we find a creative Lord able to impart to us the ideas and principles we need in any time crunch. If we give all to Him, we soon find Him a gentle master whose "yoke is easy" and whose "burden is light."

A tip on time: Whom or what do you serve? Be brutally honest. Is it pleasing others? Money? God? Making a name for yourself? Living it up? Take a few minutes now to discuss your answer with the Lord. Then determine what, if anything, you might change about it.

NOTES

1. Mark Porter, *The Time of Your Life* (Wheaton, Ill.: Victor, 1983), p. 54.
2. See article on C. T. Studd in *Dictionary of the Christian Church* (Grand Rapids, Mich.: Zondervan, 1974), p. 936.
3. In Charles R. Swindoll, *Improving Your Serve* (Waco, Tex.: Word, 1981), p. 29.
4. J. Grant Howard, *Balancing Life's Demands* (Portland, Oreg.: Multnomah, 1983), p. 68.

7

The Days Are Evil

Most people are not aware of what actually occupies their time. Yet it makes little sense to attempt to solve a problem without first assessing its nature and extent. And, as an early sage observed, a problem well stated is half solved. So with time. When we discover what we actually are doing with it, our task is half done.

—Ted Engstrom and Alec MacKenzie,
Managing Your Time

Wendell Brown, of Tacoma, Washington, had a problem in the Pierce County Assessor-Treasurer's office. Too much time on coffee breaks. Poor productivity. A backlog of paperwork. No time to plan how to make the office function better.

What did he do? He established a Quiet Time. There were to be no visitors. No talking to fellow workers. No moving around in the office.

For how long? For the first two hours of the day.

Then what did one do in that two hours? You could catch up on homework. Eliminate distractions. Plan out the day. Mr. Brown placed a "Do Not Disturb" sign on the door, and except in emergencies, the phone was disconnected.

So what has been the reaction?

One civil servant says, "It's more like kindergarten."

Another remarked that "it's wrecking morale." Everyone is "just totally discouraged. I feel awfully, awfully sorry for the taxpayers."[1]

Mr. Brown is trying to solve a problem in his office. What problem? Productivity? Morale? Getting the paperwork through?

Partly. But he has a bigger one he may not even know about. It's found in Ephesians 5:15-16: "Be very careful, then, how you live—not as unwise but as wise, making the most of every opportunity, because *the days are evil*" (italics added).

In Mr. Brown's case, he was up against more than the need for quiet and productivity. He faced the problem of human depravity and the ability of the devil to tempt, the world to beguile, and the flesh to lust. His program could succeed only as he dealt with those realities in a forthright, convincing fashion.

What then does it mean that the "days are evil"? Does it mean that time itself is evil? I don't think so. But it's one of the first principles we have to fix in our minds if we are ever to escape the time crunch.

THE CONSEQUENCES OF THE FALL

When Adam and Eve chose to eat the forbidden fruit, everything in life was affected, including time. Our days, hours, minutes, and seconds came under the power of the Evil One, Satan, as well as the worldly attitude that rejects God and the desire to please ourselves. Suddenly, time was no longer for love, joy, and peace in fellowship with the Almighty, but up for grabs to any sin-monger willing to scoop it up. We became customers at the local Sin Fairgrounds, strolling from booth to booth, looking for anything to do except what is right, good, and pleasing to God.

That the "days are evil" means they're shot through and through with the results and concerns of the mastermind of evil, Satan. My day and your day literally starts out staked with evil's claims.

Please understand. We don't just visit this Sin Fair-grounds; we're born in it. We know nothing else until we meet Jesus Christ. Everything offered in Sin Fair-grounds is worthless, fruitless, and evil. We literally have NO other choices.

That is, unless someone begins to claim—"re-deem," as Paul says in the King James Version of Ephesians 5:16—a patch of that time for the kingdom. Whether we like it or not, it is the truth that when we were unbelievers, every moment of our day was infected by evil. No matter how decent and nice we were, in God's eyes it was lost time.

When we became believers, we had the same problem. Satan prepared his agenda. There it was before us—on our desks, in our libraries, by our kitchen sinks, on our television sets, or hung from the rear view mirrors of our cars. If it were not for the guiding presence of the Spirit, we might well be Christians and still scheduling every minute for the sake of evil purpose.

Not Trying to Be Morbid

I'm not trying to be morbid about it. But our problem with time and hurry is clearly a result of the Fall and the fact that "the days are evil." Our schedules can easily become crowded with what is "evil" and not what is good and "best."

I don't mean "evil" in the sense of murder, rape, robbery, pillage, and plunder.

No, evil comes under many headings. It can range from a few minutes reading the gossip column to a couple extra hours in the sack in the morning. It includes the worst things—drunkenness, drug highs, illicit affairs, murder, and theft—to the seemingly harmless—walking around the mall, flipping through *People* magazine at the doctor's office, a romantic evening at the local bistro.

Not that these things are "evil" in themselves. In some cases, it might be God's desire and plan that we engage in those activities. Walking around the mall might provide some needed recreation, a time to be alone, and a chance to get some important shopping done. *People* magazine might be God's way of taking our minds off a problem. And the romantic evening at the bistro can provide a satisfying chance to build a marital relationship.

The question is: Why are we doing these things, and how is it affecting our commitment to build God's kingdom and love Him and our neighbors as ourselves?

THE BATTLE FOR YOUR TIME

That the days are evil means that your desire to "make the most of the opportunity" and use your time for God's will and work will be a steady battle. Wherever you stake out a claim for the kingdom, evil constantly creeps up to the edge of that claim seeking to distract you in another direction.

Furthermore, there will be no end to this battle. Satan is relentless. What we have discovered in the 1990s is really an old problem. The days were just as evil for Moses, Elijah, Jesus, Paul, and Peter as for us. Remember how in Exodus 18 Jethro advises his son-in-law Moses not to spend all his time deciding each legal case among his people? Jethro told him to appoint judges over various groupings. Otherwise, Moses would wear out.

That's a clear example of the hurried life-style. I'm certain Moses felt the same way any of our twentieth-century hurriers feel. He was "pressed for time." He felt "hassled." There was "too much to do, and too little time to do it in." If Moses continued to do things as he was doing them, he would definitely collapse. What good would he be then? But God through Jethro turned His man around with the truth. Now he could stake a new claim on his time for the kingdom.

Even Jesus encountered this problem. In Mark 1:35-39, Jesus arises to pray in the early morning. This followed a full day and night of healing, casting out demons, preaching, and discipling. Simon and the other disciples ran about trying to find Jesus. When they did find him, Simon said, "Everyone is looking for you!"

Now those people had needs. They wanted to see Jesus. If He let them, He could spend months in that one place teaching and healing everyone. But Jesus knew that the "days were evil" and that Simon's plea was only one more ploy in Satan's sack. He answered Simon, "Let us go somewhere else—to the nearby villages—so I can preach there also. That is why I have come" (Mark 1:38).

The territory was already Satan's. But Jesus carved out blocks of time here and there to redeem them for the kingdom. He did not let the reality of "the days are evil" detour or derail His mission.

IN THE WORKPLACE

I find Satan's capacity to derail a mission a constant pressure in the workplace. I'm working along, doing the tasks I know I need to get done, and suddenly I glance up at my coffee cup. *A voice rings inside my mind: Why don't you take a little break? You need to clear out your head.* Before I've even thought about it, I'm on the way to the coffee room. Half an hour later I sashay back to my desk, suddenly in a sweat because I'm behind schedule.

SO MANY PLOYS

Satan has many ploys. What are some of his best ones? Try this list:

Lack of purpose and direction in our Christian lives. If you don't have something you're shooting for, some all-important goal you're striving to reach, you'll not only never get there, but the place you *do* reach will be frustrating and unfulfilling.

Claudia Morain writes in "The Stress of Having It All," "So you've got the career, the cars, the spouse, the spa, the house, the health club, the kids, and the clothes. Trouble is you're so frantic, frazzled, overbooked, and overwhelmed you don't have time to enjoy any of it."[2]

Though she is not coming from a biblical standpoint, she could be speaking of too many of us who do. Bill Tamulonis, a young banker in Baltimore, Maryland, told me, "I realized that the things that I valued highly were getting a small proportion of my time and energy. I spent my time on earthly and material pursuits that had little eternal value."

Rich Tucker, another young businessman from Baltimore, said, "I graduated from college fifteen years ago. I was very involved in my work and progressed in the company. But I was spending as much as seventy hours a week in work, with a lot of travel. I have a nine year old son, and he was hurting. It was stressful to meet family needs and work needs."

Both of these men, through the influence of their pastor, decided to redirect their lives through discovering new purpose in serving God and His priorities.

Lack of joy in serving God. When you find no joy in what you're doing, you end up spending your time feeling angry, misused, and abused by others.

Randy Schiller, a computer consultant, put it this way: "You might get involved in solving a serious problem in the church. But what happens is that it starts to consume everything. You feel guilty. It all takes time away from other things. You begin to resent church, and soon you want to walk away and have nothing do with it anymore. The joy is gone."

Boredom. There are two kinds of boredom: boredom from not enjoying what you're doing, and boredom from not having anything to do. As a result you fritter away your time. Afterward, you spend more time feeling guilty, upset, and worthless.

Poor planning. Some say that if you fail to plan, you plan to fail. Planning saves time. You don't have to do the job again and again by trial and error. You get it right the first time by thinking it through ahead of time.

Planning extends to all of the details of life, even planning "wasted time." Woody Price, a recent graduate of Geneva College in Pennsylvania, said, "I find myself blowing off time haphazardly, instead of constructively planning rest periods."

Charles Hummel says in *Tyranny of the Urgent*, "The modern businessman recognizes the principle of taking time out for evaluation. When Greenwalt was president of DuPont, he said, 'One minute spent in planning saves three or four minutes in execution.'"[3]

If goals, priorities, and "taking joy in what you do" are keys to success in taming the time crunch, evaluation is the bolt and lock.

"Most people are not aware of what actually occupies their time," Ted Engstrom and Alec MacKenzie observe in their book *Managing Your Time*. "Yet it makes little sense to attempt to solve a problem without first assessing its nature and extent. And, as an early sage observed, a problem well stated is half solved. So with time. When we discover what we actually are doing with it, our task is half done."[4]

Not living within our limits. If we spend too much, as Eileen Merrell told me, we'll have to spend more time making it up. Similarly, if we overschedule, someone will make us pay the price. Brent Brooks, the church planter I mentioned earlier, said, "A hard lesson I've had to learn is that I'm not omnipotent, and I'm not omnipresent." But too many of us act as if we're trying to be.

Mary Ann Dean saw it this way: "I [had] learned to work and volunteer to gain acceptance. I felt compelled to please others." Then she read a book called *Another Chance*, by Sharon Wegscheider (Science and Behavior Books, 1981). It changed her approach to life. "I gained insight into being the oldest child and how I felt I had to carry the family problems. What a time sapper! Each family member is responsible for his or her life and set of problems. One person can't carry it all."

Foolish pleasures and entertainments. Our world is full of them. There's a live act on every corner, entertainment par excellence down the block at the video store or on the tube, and something for everyone else in the local mall. Sure it's worldliness. But it's hard to resist. And it eats up those hours—fast.

Laziness in setting priorities. Watson Pindell, a man over eighty who has served as a school principal and as a college president, remarked, "My problems are mainly ones of laziness rather than time." He told me, "No human being who is really living has enough time. On the other hand, we prodigally waste the time we have. We spend too much time on admittedly unimportant tasks."

The unimportant and urgent will often take away from the important and not so urgent. We need to learn to make distinctions with how we use our time.

High expectations/low returns. Discouragement is a prime time-waster. You get down in the dumps so far you can't get up and go. But discouragement often comes from having high expectations that are never realized. We get our expectations not from the word of God, as we should, but from our culture, our greed, our pride. That always ends in the pit.

The name of this situation is burnout. In an article in the *Wall Street Journal,* "Stepping Off the Fast Track," Carol Hymowitz reports that "psychologists say they're seeing more and more younger men who are suffering burnout . . .

"'They come in with symptoms like hypochondria, sleep disorders and depression,' says Susan Price, a New York psychotherapist. 'When they start talking, they admit the emphasis they've placed on being successful and making a huge amount of money hasn't made them very happy.'"[5]

Procrastination. By putting off today what we can do "sometime" we may actually be creating a bigger time killer than we think. If you put off checking the oil in your crankcase, your car engine may burn up. If you put off making up that report for your boss, you may end up having to do it in too short a time, and doing it poorly, or incorrectly. Which means doing it over. Which means more wasted time.

Clutter. The bigger the mess, the happier Satan is. You can't find things and must spend long hours looking through stuff because you were disorganized.

A pastor's wife told me, "I don't have enough time by virtue of my personality. I tend to be very unorganized. I have to make a conscious effort to get organized."

What happens is that the house doesn't get cleaned the way it should. It becomes hard to find things amidst the clutter. There are long searches through unorganized files to find the simplest papers.

I find this is true in my workplace. If we let the filing go for one week and the clutter builds up, someone may have to spend an extra hour shuffling through papers to find an important document.

This was even true of a simple thing like my key chain. It was disorganized—no order to the keys. As a result, I often had to spend minutes in the dark trying to find my house or car key. What I did was reorder the keys so that certain ones were on the ends, and each was ordered so I could find it quickly. It works beautifully.

Clutter steals time. Being organized always helps.

Perfectionism. You've got to get it so perfect that you end up frazzling not only yourself, but everyone else.

Eileen Merrell commented, "The basic truth for my time crunch was that I was trying to do it all. I tried to look in total control, not wanting to ask my husband for help. Yet, I was angry that he didn't. (How could he

know? He couldn't read my mind!) After asking, his loving response was tremendous."

That's a kind of perfectionism, always thinking you
can go it alone, do it yourself, be independent. But it's
the essence of rejection of God and the world He has
created, which is an interdependent "help me and I'll
help you" world.

A man I know is the complete perfectionist. He goes
over and over a thing—a report, a letter, a speech—until
he thinks it's perfect. Then he finds something else
wrong with it! Although what he ends up with is often
very good, there is a point of diminishing returns. Finding that point and keeping within its limits is part of
beating the time crunch.

Failure to delegate. You're not always the best person for the job. But you may be able to pick the best one.

Gordon MacDonald says, "I know many Christian
leaders who will candidly admit that they spend up to
80 percent of their time doing things at which they are
second-best. For example, my strongest gift is in the
area of preaching and teaching. While I am a reasonably
good administrator, that is certainly not the best arrow
in my pastoral quiver.

"So why did I spend almost 75 percent of my available time trying to administrate and relatively little
time doing the necessary study and preparation for
good sermons when I was younger?"[6]

It was only when he learned to delegate and give
others a place in his ministry that MacDonald found
any semblance of true freedom and balance.

Poor management of the time we have. Though time
is not a commodity to be managed, but an environment
in which we live, we still have to order ourselves and
our use of it. The Lord told us to do all things "in a fitting and orderly way" (1 Corinthians 14:40). That goes
for the individual as well as the church.

Woody Price told me that he likes to use a "Day
Timer," one of those precious tools many of us do with-

out, but really can't. "Mental planning doesn't work," he says. Why? "You forget things, you get off on something else, a tangent." His study of how computer systems work has helped him use his time more efficiently.

He feels that without such tools, we can easily commit ourselves at times to things that we shouldn't, or which, in the long run, don't prove as valuable and productive.

Inattention to prevention. Taking preventive measures is an important time saver. Anyone who has run out of gas on the highway knows the problem of inattention to prevention. All that time walking down the highway in search of a gas can and a gas station forces us to consider: "Will I prevent this from happening again by some forethought and planning, or not?"

Recently, a friend went to the doctor with severe warts on her feet. The doctor took one look and said, "Why didn't you come sooner?"

Her response, "I hoped they would go away."

He shook his head. "If you had come sooner, all this would have been prevented. Now as it is, we've got a long hard fight ahead of us." And higher doctor bills, more time in the doctor's office, more forms to fill out, and so on, and on.

Such a simple thing as getting the snow shovel or umbrella before the big snow or rain saves the time of standing in the store with the hundreds of others who failed to plan in advance and take preventive measures. Many things in life, from regular medical and dental checkups to turning off the outside water before winter, are preventive and save time in the long run.

Worry. What an incredible time-killer! Yet many Christians spend their lives locked in by worry. Some are immobilized entirely by their incessant turning over of the possibilities.

An old joke pictures a coat-maker named Lieberman who suffered from terrible insomnia. His partner advised him to count sheep. "It's the best cure ever," he said. Lieberman replied, "What can I lose?" He decided to try it that night.

The next morning he looked more haggard than ever. "What on earth happened?" asked his partner. Lieberman replied, "Well, I counted the sheep. I got up to fifty thousand. Then I sheared the sheep and made up fifty thousand coats. Beautiful ones. But then came the problem that kept me awake all night: where was I going to get fifty thousand linings?"

That's a joke, yet not far from the truth. Like Mark Twain said, "I am an old man and have known a great many troubles, but most of them never happened!"

Ignorance of basic time-saving techniques. Michael Green said, "I could show you how to organize your time in thirty minutes." But many people never learn the basics. There are a multitude of books out there about simple steps to organizing and managing our time. But we don't take advantage of them, to our own frustration and loss.

Lila Williamson, a home-worker and career woman in Annapolis, Maryland, told me, "Most recently, the crush of time affected me in that for ten months I accepted a special project job in Washington, D.C., commuting seventy miles a day. I left early in the morning and got home about 7:00 P.M. Choir on Wednesdays was at 7:30. I had no time for myself. I ate supper, did dishes, walked the dog, and it was time to get ready for bed and the next day, and the cycle continued. Time was a premium."

She could easily have been stymied had she not cultivated some excellent time-saving habits. "What I did was use the time to read and pray as I rode on the commuter bus. I caught up on a lot of reading. All to say, when God rearranges our lives, we need to seek His will in that situation and use it as best we can."

I have recently been learning the power of the simple "To Do" list in the context of my computerized work situation. We have a program on our network called

"Higgins Productivity Software." In it, the first thing that comes onto our screen—automatically—is our schedule. We don't have to waste time spinning gears or wondering what job to tackle first. It's all there.

Ignorance of the divine line on time. This is by far the biggest time killer. We spend our time in useless, non-kingdom pursuits. It may seem like we're accomplishing something at the time, but in the end we may it wasn't so worthwhile. Woody Price told me, "I find myself doing a lot of things that I see as important at the time but really are not. This is because I wish to do those things and not the things that are really important."

Here's a chart that might help you zero in on some kingdom versus non-kingdom pursuits:

Kingdom Pursuit	Non-kingdom Activity
1. Visiting the sick	Visiting the mall
2. Helping a friend redo his recreation room	Watching Monday Night Football
3. Singing in the choir	Singing in a secular group
4. Going to church, giving, teaching, and so on	Going to the Moose Lodge
5. Spending time with your kids, wife, family, relatives	Spending time watching videos
6. Witnessing	Telling "jokes" and stories
7. Bible study	Reading "romantic" novels
8. Prayer in the car	Listening to secular music tapes in the car
9. Reading solid, God-honoring books	Reading big, sexy novels
10. Listening to God-honoring music and speaking tapes	Listening to secular tapes

Of course, any one of the above "non-kingdom" activities could easily be turned into a "kingdom" activity if it was linked to a kingdom activity, such as building relationships that will lead to love, giving, and witness. But the point is that most of the "non-kingdom" activities listed above can easily amount to wasted time. Even when used for recreation, there are ways to find kingdom pursuits that can also be relaxational and recreational.

Plain old everyday sin. Spell it any way you like. From the latest Action thriller to Zap Comics, a lot of it is just plain sin. We're still embedded in the world, with little desire to get out.

HE USES EVERY ONE

It is a sharp-edged picture we have given of the "evil days" that Satan foists upon us. But that is the reality we must attack.

But is there any hope? Absolutely. Satan, though evil and powerful, is not sovereign and all-powerful. And there is Someone Else on our side who is.

A tip on time: Look at the day that has just passed. What parts of it would you say were affected by evil? Why do you think evil took over at that point? What might you do differently?

NOTES

1. Richard B. Schmitt, "Now If We Could Only Get Them to Keep Quiet for 22 More Hours," *Wall Street Journal*, September 5, 1989, p. B1.
2. Claudia Morain, "The Stress of Having It All," *Washington Post*, September 22, 1988, p. C5.
3. Charles E. Hummel, *Tyranny of the Urgent* (Carol Stream, Ill.: InterVarsity, 1967), p. 12.
4. Ted W. Engstrom and R. Alec Mackenzie, *Managing Your Time* (Grand Rapids, Mich.: Zondervan, 1967), p. 57.
5. Carol Hymowitz, "Stepping Off the Fast Track," *Wall Street Journal*, June 13, 1989, p. B1.
6. Gordon MacDonald, *Ordering Your Private World* (Nashville, Tenn.: Thomas Nelson, 1984), p. 82.

8

A Time for Everything
Under the Sun

Though I am always in haste, I am never in a hurry,
because I never undertake more work than I can go
through with calmness of spirit.
—John Wesley

In preparation for writing this book, I sent out more than one hundred and fifty questionnaires. About forty came back. My contacts gave me a multitude of interesting and illustrative answers to my questions. But two stood out for their brevity.

One was from an editor who stuck a yellow post-it-note to the front of my questionnaire. She wrote, "I hate to say it, Mark, but I don't have time to fill this out!"

Touché!

The second was from Haddon Robinson, president of Conservative Baptist Seminary in Denver, Colorado. He wrote, "I'm sure that what I have learned is found in a score of books on time management. One thing I have discovered, however, is that if you're a morning person, no crisis worth its salt takes place before eleven o'clock in the morning!"

In other words, many of those things rearing their ugly heads as "crises" are nothing of the sort. People simply hype them into crises because they want what they want when they want it.

Still, to hitchhike on an old saying about the subject, "There's a time for everything and everything has its time." I don't resent the fact that neither of these people had time to fill out my questionnaire. I'm just glad they returned it. I can't expect my concerns to become their priorities just because I sent them a form letter I had cranked out on a computer faster than it took for them to write out their brief answers!

AN IMPORTANT PRINCIPLE

But beyond this I see another important principle about time that relates to the God who is sovereign over all of time. It is found in Ecclesiastes 3:1, 11: "There is a time for everything, and a season for every activity under heaven. . . . He has made everything beautiful in its time. He has also set eternity in the hearts of men; yet they cannot fathom what God has done from beginning to end."

When Solomon used the word *season* in verse one, he used a word that means an "appointed time, a planned time for an activity."[1] That means there's a purpose behind everything that happens. It's not only appointed in the sense of "fixed," but it's backed by the wisdom, love, and goodness of God Himself. He has appointed for a purpose all times and all things that happen. Verse 11 reveals something even more incredible in the word *beautiful*. The Hebrew term behind it literally means *beautiful*, but it also means *excellent*.[2] God has made everything "beautiful even excellent in its own time."

That says something even more illustrative. God's work in creation and history is perfect. Even though evil permeates every nook and cranny of the universe, God somehow—to those who love and follow Him—makes it all beautiful and appropriate.

I'm convinced that at the end of history, when eternity has begun, all the redeemed from every age will see the wisdom and perfection of God's plan in human events. They will marvel that even the bad things have turned out to have been a means ultimately to draw us to Him in intimacy and love.

That's not to say evil things are good. Not at all. But it means that God has arranged our lives so that everything is appropriate in its time. The opportunities, circumstances, problems, and situations of life plunk down in our path at the appropriate moment, neither too soon, nor too late.

A VISION OF GOD'S SOVEREIGNTY

In approaching the subject of time, hurry, and the helter-skelter life-style so many of us lead, we have to reckon with the truth of God's sovereignty. Everything that happens is ultimately under His control and part of the grand design that will complete His eternal plan. Whatever is happening in our lives now, however time-crunched or harried, can all turn out for good—if we submit to the Lord who is the sovereign over time.

John Wesley knew this truth well. He wrote more than 40,000 sermons in his life and traveled some 250,000 miles by horseback. That works out to be about two sermons and twelve and a half miles on horse per day every day from his conversion at Aldersgate on May 24, 1738, to his death in 1791. That's an incredible accomplishment.

Yet, he rarely seemed in a hurry. He wrote, "Though I am always in haste, I am never in a hurry, because I never undertake more work than I can go through with calmness of spirit."

As we gain this vision of God's sovereignty, we're set free. It's no longer necessary to rush. The God who rules time and loves us is a God of rest, who has made all things "beautiful" in their time. True beauty can't be taken in at a glance. It must be savored, enjoyed, experienced to its fullness. To paraphrase someone else, "God has given us time to stop and smell the roses, but it's up to us to stop and smell!"

THE BEAUTY OF GOD'S SOVEREIGNTY

The sovereignty of God is one of the most important and hope-building doctrines of the Bible when it comes to our problem with time. It means:

1. All events are under His control (Psalm 33:11-12; Isaiah 45:5-7).
2. He has allowed those events on the basis of omniscience, perfect wisdom, unchanging love, and infinite holiness (Psalm 103:8; 1 Peter 1:16-17).
3. Whatever events occur have His purpose behind them (Ephesians 1:11-12).
4. He can "work" even evil events "together for good" (Romans 8:28; see KJV).

This is why Solomon could say everything is "beautiful" in its time. Even our present time crunch is "beautiful." How so? Perhaps to force us to learn His principles and truth about time so that we can change and use it for His kingdom.

NEGATIVE BEFORE POSITIVE

Don't you find that God often allows us to experience the negative before we can know the positive? He sets us eating the wilted grass on evil's side of the fence before He lets us hop over to claim those greener tufts. It's part of His way of motivating us to choose the good. By experiencing evil we soon find how repulsive it is. Thus, when we finally choose the good, we're not inclined to go back.

BALANCING TWO ELEMENTS

Learning to live within the confines of God's beautiful time calls for a balancing of two important elements: timing and scheduling.

We're all familiar with scheduling. That's the process of making an appointment, setting a time and date for something you want to happen. Mark Porter says in *The Time of Your Life*, "Scheduling is an important part of 20th-century business. Schedules and deadlines give an urgency to activities that might otherwise drag."[3]

But if you're not careful, your schedule can soon become your God. You become inflexible, rigid, and isolated by the dictates of your priorities.

What if God's plan calls for a kingdom opportunity to invade your schedule? You might regard His "gift" as an intrusion.

TIMING

That brings up the issue of timing. William T. McConnell sees timing as of paramount importance in his book *The Gift of Time*.

> Timing refers to the arranging of things in order, or the coming together of events in a fortuitous way. It is the "right time" or "appropriate season" so common in the Bible. Scheduling is also a way of putting things in order, but it does so by keeping them separate, not bringing them together. "By scheduling we compartmentalize; this makes it possible to concentrate on one thing at a time, but it also deprives us of context."
>
> When we equate the schedule, the linear order of events, with life itself, our view of reality shrinks and thought itself becomes divided into segmented compartments. The difference between biblical timing and secular scheduling is the difference between our ideas "in the wild" and in our own zoo. Caged ideas are much easier to study and organize, but they lose their vigor and excitement.[4]

It's scheduling that helps us get our work done on time; it's God's timing in bringing to us the beautiful things in life that gets our work done with joy, fulfillment, and meaning. Only in His timing is there the possibility of real living. As Adlai Stevenson said, "In the

long run it is not the years in your life but the life in
your years that counts."

Better Understanding

Lila Williamson amplifies the idea. She told me,
"We don't really manage our time in God's hands, but
He manages the time in our lives. He often takes our
time because He wants to use us in someone else's life.
Now if our schedules are so busy that God doesn't have
room, He just may use someone else."

God's timing means that the opportunities and
people-needs that collide with our schedules may need
to take precedence. Only discerning hearts can determine if a present need should take precedence over a
planned event or action. The only way we can get such
discernment is through reliance on God through study
of His word and prayer.

A Vivid Picture

Ramona Tucker, an editor with Harold Shaw Publishers in Wheaton, Illinois, gave me a vivid example of
the interaction between human scheduling and God's
timing. She said, "Our house has been a revolving door
for teens and singles into their thirties. We've had teens
live with us who have problems (sexual abuse for one)
for months at a time. And I've discovered what being a
working mother feels like while having a teen who needs
you at home. We've been through court systems and all
the ups and downs with our 'kids.' We are writing our
second book together on the subject now. (And my third.)"

That's God's timing.

How, then, do they cope? "The phone is turned off
at 10:00 P.M. every night now. We have an answering
machine. We can hear the message, so we know if it is
urgent. Thanks to technology we don't have to be phone
addicts (our phone rings constantly). After 10:00 P.M.
each night is our 'couple time' and also we wake up at
5:30 A.M. for 'couple' time, then eat breakfast together.

"After my husband leaves, I indulge in Bible reading, then memorize a nugget while I walk in my neighborhood for fifteen minutes. After that I practice the
piano to cool down from my walk. Finally, I take a
shower, and I'm at work by 8:00! It works marvelously."
You can see the timing and scheduling principle.
Though her schedule is fairly compact and straightfor-
ward, there is room for interruptions and "opportunities" that God may place in her path.

An Exhortation

If you find interruptions and people-needs a constant intrusion on your time, the first step is to reckon
with God's sovereignty. Could He, in His love and wisdom, be sending these folks and needs your way because
He wants you to minister to them? Or are they genuine
"evil" intrusions that you have to deal with by refusing
to give them your time and energy?

Only a realistic waiting on and seeking of God, a
consistent walk with Him, will help you see the difference. If we put everything off in lieu of our exalted
"schedule," we may miss His "beautiful" seasons. On
the other hand, if we never schedule anything, we may
not get anything done.

As an old gravestone says:

> He walked beneath the moon
> and slept beneath the sun.
> He lived a life of going to do
> and died with nothing done.[5]

A Question

But at this point we have to ask: What's it all for?
Where is God taking us?

This is the issue of God's goals for history, as well
as us individually. We'll look at that next.

A tip on time: How do you view the sovereignty of God in relation to your problems with time? Do you find any comfort in it? Why or why not? Take a moment and talk to the Lord about what He can do to help you find the "beauty" in your days.

NOTES

1. Brown, Driver, and Briggs, *Hebrew and English Lexicon of the Old Testament* (London: Oxford U. Press, 1907), pp. 772-73.
2. Ibid., p. 421.
3. Mark Porter, *The Time of Your Life* (Wheaton, Ill.: Victor, 1983), p. 131.
4. William T. McConnell, *The Gift of Time* (Downers Grove, Ill.: InterVarsity, 1983), p. 52.
5. Porter, p. 144.

9

God's Goals

Come, follow me . . and I will make you fishers of men.

—Mark 1:17

William T. McConnell zeroes in on the prime issue of time with these penetrating words: "For the short haul, [Alan] Lakein [author of the best-selling book *How to Get Control of Your Time and Your Life*] and the evangelical time managers are quite right. Their techniques work. You can get an amazing amount done, eliminate time wasters and 'find time' for a horde of things you have wanted to do. . . .

"Sooner or later, however, if we are even a bit reflective, we may wonder if we are heading toward the right objective. Are our goals really what are significant in life? It is an agonizing moment; we may discover that the short-range goals we have set for ourselves are not really our own, but are just a reflection of society's rootless values, or else that all we have done is dedicated to our own egos. Our goals may prove to be nothing more than a 'game plan' drawn up without really knowing the object of the game."[1]

GOD'S GOALS

The organized Christian has goals. He's going somewhere, for something. But what for? And why? And what about God's goals?

Sooner or later, we must come to grips with the question, What truly does God want of me? What are His plans, His purpose, His goals for my life, for our lives?

It is "an agonizing moment," as McConnell says.

A DREAM

Before I became a Christian, I remember having a vivid encounter with my own conscience. For some months I had been reading the Bible and praying, even though I had not yet come to know the Lord Jesus personally.

One day I was lying on my bed in my fraternity house thinking about the events of my day. Certain things that I had done came into my mind and stirred within me a vague feeling of guilt. It was a feeling I'd lived with for a long time and had never resolved.

As my mind roved over the facts of my life, I was suddenly aware of a searing sense of conviction about a number of personal sins. This thought was in my mind: *What if there really is a God and He has seen me doing that? What will happen to me?*

In those few minutes I looked back over my life. Though I hadn't ever done anything particularly heinous, neither had I accomplished anything very worthwhile. My mind filled with a vivid picture of a person whose life was a waste, everything piled on a stinking garbage heap—fit only for throwing out.

All my life up to that point I had struggled with questions: What mattered? What happened when you died? Did you face God? What would He do with all your faults and sins? And most of all, What was I supposed to do with my life?

It was only a few months later that I experienced a cleansing and freeing encounter with Jesus. It was a total and transforming turnaround. Everything in life suddenly became related to Jesus, His program, His purpose, His reality. I pored over scripture like an FBI expert over a master criminal's fingerprints. I went to worship services, Bible studies, and fellowships like a man in love. I lived for knowing, walking with, and experiencing the person of Jesus. Nothing else mattered.

But those were more simplified days. I was single. I stood at the beginning of a career, and more schooling. My time was my own. I had few liabilities and responsibilities.

CHANGES

Now, as a husband, father, manager in a company, writer, speaker, and church member, things don't look as simple as "knowing, walking with, and experiencing the person of Jesus." There's just a lot more to life, in life, and about life that crowd my attention span—and many more people crying for my time, effort, and resources.

We have to face the question: Where is God taking me—and you?

JESUS SPELLED OUT A GOAL AT THE START

When Jesus called Andrew, Peter, James, and John to follow Him, He told them one of His goals for their lives: "Come, follow me . . . and I will make you fishers of men" (Mark 1:17). That was enough vision and direction for those four men to leave everything behind and follow Him. Management experts repeatedly preach the need to establish similar goals for our lives. "Where are you headed? What are you trying to do?" One of my professors used to say, "If you don't know where you're going, you'll hit it every time!"

But our personal goals are useless if they're not somehow bound up with God's goals and purposes for

His creation—because ultimately His goals will be established and completed. Everyone else's will lie dashed in the dust.

I was once in a ministry in which my goals were contrary to my employer's. We argued it out over and over. I was convinced I was right. I saw my goals as better, more reachable, and more in line with the truth. But he was my employer, and one day he told me to start looking for another job.

In the same way, Satan and his forces are battling God and His angels for control of the universe. Satan says, "My goals are better. Follow me and we'll win."

Beneath Satan we see each person in this world shaking his fist in God's face and crying, "I will do as I please!"

In the meantime, God laughs at them all (Psalm 2:4). He has installed His King on Zion and He advises us, "Kiss the Son, lest he be angry and you be destroyed in your way, for his wrath can flare up in a moment. Blessed are all who take refuge in him" (Psalm 2:12).

No matter how great, lofty, and certain our goals are in this world, if they are not in line with God's ultimate purpose, they are doomed.

What, then, are God's goals?

THREE MAJOR GOALS

There are at least three major goals God has revealed in Scripture. The first is *to manifest the glory of God.*

God will not "give [His] glory to another" (Isaiah 42:8). "Nevertheless, as surely as I live and as surely as *the glory of the Lord fills the whole earth . . .*" (Numbers 14:21*a*).

God's glory is the sum total of all that He is and all that makes Him worthy of worship, love, reverence, and obedience. It's all He has created (angels, the universe, everything), all that He is (His character and person), and all that He does (salvation of man, mighty works, sanctification).

Why does He want to manifest His glory?

1. That all creation might know His glory (Numbers 14:21)
2. That all creation might love and enjoy Him (John 4:22-24)
3. That all creation might receive His gifts (John 10:10)

If God's first goal is to make known His glory to all creation, then somehow whatever we do in life must incorporate that goal. We must set aside time to know and enjoy Him, and to receive His good gifts. When we pray in the Lord's prayer, "Hallowed be Thy name," we are agreeing that He should be glorified by all people.

The second goal is *to establish His kingdom in His creation.*

The angel Gabriel told Mary that Jesus' "kingdom will never end" (Luke 1:33). Jesus told His disciples that "all authority in heaven and on earth has been given to me" (Matthew 28:18). Paul was confident that the Lord would bring him "safely to his heavenly kingdom" (2 Timothy 4:18).

Ever since Satan rose up in rebellion against God, the Lord Almighty has been reestablishing His kingdom over creation.

What is involved in establishing His kingdom? At least six activities:

1. Preaching the gospel to every person (Matthew 28:18-20)
2. The salvation of sinners (Luke 19:10)
3. The sanctification of the saints (Romans 8:29)
4. The completion of world history (1 Corinthians 15:23-29)

5. The eradication of evil (Revelation 20:11-15)
6. The beginning of eternity in a perfect universe
   (2 Peter 3:13; Revelation 21-22)

Again, this is where God is headed. When we pray in the Lord's prayer, "Thy kingdom come," we are agreeing about all of these points. His goal is our goal. Thus, whatever personal goals we have, they must somehow coincide with some or all of God's goals.

God's third goal is *to carry out His eternal plan for His creation*. Before anything else ever was, God made up a plan by which He would do two things:

1. Manifest His glory
2. Establish His kingdom

Everything that happens in life is working toward that end. That plan includes everything that happens —good, evil, and neutral. God does not cause evil, but His plan includes it and works around it when it occurs.

When we pray, "Thy will be done," in the Lord's prayer, we're actually agreeing with His goal to carry out His eternal plan. We're saying, "We want to be part of what You have planned and willed. We want to be in conformity with Your will."

OUR GOALS OR GOD'S GOALS?

Sooner or later, we all decide whose plan and program we're in. If we choose our own goals, then we will plan and schedule our time according to those goals. But if we align our goals with God and go His way, another outlook takes over.

Thus, in determining personal goals we must consider—almost brutally—how they relate to God's goals. If they have nothing to do with them, why are we establishing such goals to begin with?

A tip on time: As you consider the goals God has for His creation, which ones are most significant to you? Why? What do you see that is happening in your life now that contributes to the accomplishment of that goal?

NOTE

1. William T. McConnell, *The Gift of Time* (Downers Grove, Ill.: InterVarsity, 1983), p. 56.

10

We Are His Workmanship

[God] seems to do nothing of Himself which He can possibly delegate to His creatures. He commands us to do slowly and blunderingly what He could do perfectly and in the twinkling of an eye.

Creation seems to be delegation through and through. I suppose this is because He is a giver.

—C. S. Lewis

When *Time* magazine's article "How America Has Run Out of Time," appeared in April 1989, many people were quick to agree with *Time*'s assessment.

But not everyone.

Robert J. Samuelson of *Newsweek* took quite a different view. "Just about everyone seems to think that Americans are more harried and short of time than ever," he says. "Well, we aren't. This is a psycho-fact. We feel it, and therefore it must be. Feeling and fact are assumed to be the same. If Americans think they're exceptionally harassed, then they are."[1]

Samuelson went on to say, "It's a myth. There has never been enough time for us. There probably never will be. Our culture is uneasy with idleness—and uneasy with that unease. As de Tocqueville long ago noted, we Americans live in constant fear that something good in life will pass us by. Consider the complaint of Donald Trump. He goes to parties or dinners four or five nights a week, but listen to him gripe. 'I hate going out on Sundays,' he once said. 'I don't like going out on Monday nights. . . . I'm not sure I like going out any night.'"

Is Samuelson sympathetic to this condition? Not at all. He retorts, "So stay home, Donald. Of all people, you can afford to relax. What's to miss?"

THE PRESSURE IS REAL

Nonetheless, Samuelson recognizes that time pressures are real. There's congested traffic out there. Working parents suffer the squeeze. People feel trampled on, used, harassed.

But facts are facts. Here are a few Samuelson cites:

Fact #1: The length of our workday is actually shorter, in relative terms. "At the turn of the century," Samuelson says, "the average working day was in the neighborhood of 10 hours, six days a week." Laundry could take a whole day because you had to use tubs and washboards. "Mass retirement didn't come into its own until the 1960s. In 1947 nearly half of men over 65 worked; in 1960 it was still a third. By 1987 only 15 percent of men over 65 (and 11 percent of all elderly) worked."

Maybe we're not as bad off as we thought!

Fact #2: Our leisure time has increased. A study done by sociologist James P. Robinson of the University of Maryland reports that "since 1965 sleeping time (about 8 hours) and eating time (an hour and a third) have remained stable." Moreover, "free time . . . is up about 10 percent to 5.5 hours a day."

Fact #3: Our time at work has actually decreased. There are more women on the job, but "since 1965 men's weekly hours have decreased from 49 to 42; women's from 39 to 31."

Fact #4: Men are doing more housework than ever. "In 1965 women did nearly six times as much (27 hours versus 4.6 hours a week [for men]). By 1985 the ratio was 2-to-1 (19.5 to 9.8 hours)." Samuelson concludes,

"Is all the rushing about good for us? Who knows? But it's thoroughly American. What's happening today is a new expression of an old condition. Striving and struggling are part of our culture. We're a hustle-bustle society. Maybe that means we're too uptight and unreflective. But time isn't flying. We are."

Nothing Has Changed

As Solomon said, "There's nothing new under the sun." Maybe our time crunch is nothing different from that of our parents. And their parents. And their parents. Undoubtedly, Adam occasionally said to Eve when she asked him to take out the garbage, "Sorry, I don't have time right now, babe." And he lived 930 years!

How We Spend Our Time

But whether you feel crunched or not, the issue is how you're using the time you have. You may be surprised how it works out in the long run. Mark Porter provides an apt chart in his book *The Time of Your Life*.[2] If we live seventy-five years, this is how we'd normally spend it:

	Activity	Percentage of Your Time
23	of 75 years sleeping	31
19	years working	25
9	years watching TV or other amusements	12
7½	years in dressing and personal care	10
6	years eating	8
6	years traveling	8
½	year worshiping and praying	0.7

This chart can put some wrinkles under your eyes and some more hurry in your step. It's genuinely scary.

What will God reward me for—twenty-three years of sleeping? Seven and a half years of dressing? Good grief!

A GOOD WORD

This is where another good word from the Book is helpful. It's found in Ephesians 2:10: "For we are God's workmanship, created in Christ Jesus to do good works, which God prepared in advance for us to do."

This verse draws together three important thoughts about the God in whose time we live. How does God intend to fulfill His goals in our lives? Consider several thoughts.

WE ARE HIS WORKMANSHIP

The English word *workmanship* is the translation of the Greek word *poema*[3] from which we get the word *poem.* In effect, we're God's poem.

But what's a poem? It's a word picture describing some mighty and artful thought, idea, or truth. In other words, we're God's living artwork.

I hope that opens some new landscapes in your mind about being created in God's image. Not only are we created in His image generically, in a general sense, but in another sense, each of us is a specific and individual creation of God, designed to show some special facet of His nature.

Think of it this way. Wallace Stevens, the American poet of the early 1900s, once wrote a poem called "Thirteen Ways of Looking at a Blackbird." That poem contains thirteen quick cameo word pictures, all directed at the subject of "black birdness." It's like thirteen photos, each of which brings out a new thought about what it means to be a blackbird.

In the same way, each of our lives is designed to bring out and display several if not many aspects of God's nature. An athlete could exemplify the power of self-discipline and diligence. A nurse might epitomize compassion. A writer could show off His intensity, logic, and depth of feeling. Each of us in some way portrays an element of His nature. That's His artwork, His workmanship in creation.

INDISPENSABLE

But there's something else. No single one of us can ever fully manifest all the elements of God's being. Thus, God works in each one of us to sculpt some special portrayal of His being that no one else in all of history ever could. In other words, we're not only unique and important but in a sense we are also indispensable. God has chosen us for a special mission that we alone can fulfill.

That means that when it comes to the problem of time we needn't hurry about trying to do everything. Rather, we can concentrate on those things for which He's made us and forget all the rest. God has someone else to do them.

HIS!

Notice also that we are *His* workmanship. Who is He? The sovereign, holy, wise, loving, and gracious God, among other things. That He is sovereign means every moment of our life is under His authority and control. Nothing can touch our lives—no situation, no time crunch, no problem—that He hasn't allowed to be there. Everything is designed for His plan and purpose. We can trust, then, that He is capable of leading us out of a time-crunched and into a time-controlled situation—if we'll let Him.

That He is holy means what He works in us will be holy. He will guide us to make a holy, godly, and righteous use of our time if we're submitted to Him. That guarantees that it's possible to bring our time under the control of the Spirit and to use it for His glory.

That He is wise means that the situation in which we find ourselves is the plan of an infinitely wise Person. Perhaps He's allowed a time crunch in our lives to lead us to greater maturity. He has planned every moment of our lives with compassionate and unrelenting wisdom. Everything that happens can enrich and develop us as people.

Moreover, it means that He can impart that wisdom to us. With His wisdom, we can learn to use the time we have in a wise, skillful manner.

That He is loving suggests that our circumstances and time problems have been allowed by a heart of love. They're all designed to benefit us. The time crunch can become a cause for rejoicing because it will build character and uprightness into our lives as well as show us the way out.

Finally, that He is gracious means He not only has the resources to help us get beyond the time crunch but is inclined to give them to us for free. Whatever we need to get our lives under control, He is all too willing to give.

The conclusion of all this is a potent truth. That we are His workmanship ultimately means He has put us where we are for wise, good, holy, loving, and gracious reasons. Just as He allowed us to walk into it for reasons known only to Him, so He also knows how to lead us out of it—and in the process make us stronger, more mature Christians.

I believe this takes the sting out of the realization that each of us will spend seven and a half years dressing and doing personal things. It means that God planned it that way, and we're only cooperating with His plan when we engage in those activities. That we'll sleep twenty-three years isn't bothersome. It's His good rest. It's His way of restoring us so that the other times will be even more fruitful. After all, as Psalm 127 (NASB*) declares, "He gives to His beloved even in his sleep." When the house is God's workmanship, there's nothing to fear. It's sound, and it will last forever.

New American Standard Bible.

C. S. Lewis understood well this thought when he said, "[God] seems to do nothing of Himself which He can possibly delegate to His creatures. He commands us to do slowly and blunderingly what He could do perfectly and in the twinkling of an eye.

"Creation seems to be delegation through and through. I suppose this is because He is a giver."[4]

One of my teachers used to say that life is like a poker game. Some are dealt good hands, but they play poorly and lose. Others receive poor hands, but they play skillfully and win.

That we are His workmanship means that no matter what hand we've been dealt, we can still win the game by submitting to Him. That's the power of His workmanship—working in and through us rather than above and beyond us.

His Purpose Is Good Works

Paul goes on to say that we are "created in Christ Jesus to do good works." What are good works? Opportunities to heal, build up, create, help, love, and rejoice; to be peaceful, gentle, faithful, self-controlled. Anything done for Him and in His name is a good work. Whether it's throwing a Frisbee and enjoying His good creation, or feeding a leprous man in Calcutta, life is to be full of good works. If you ever ask, "What should I do now?" there's always a simple answer: do something good.

The key word is "opportunity." Sometimes people speak of luck, fate, and "how the chips fall." But the truth is that God has studded each life with opportunities that "He planned beforehand." With a submissive, opportunity-grasping outlook, no life need be humdrum or hurried. Rather, this person stays on the lookout, rising up to greet each opportunity God brings his way with verve, nerve, and faith.

Whenever we desire to do such works, God provides the time. It's part of His plan. No wise planner would schedule too many things to do in too short a time.

Of course, then the question becomes: If this is so, why am I so time-crunched? There can only be one reason: you're involved in things planned by "the evil one" rather than the good God!

Some might say that's simplistic. But ultimately, how you use your time is a matter of choices (which we'll look at in the next section). If we choose the wrong things, inevitably we'll find ourselves hurried, harassed, and hard put to meet God's opportunities with anything resembling joy.

STRUGGLE AND VICTORY

Dr. Joseph Werner, whom I quoted in earlier chapters, struggled to find more time for ministry in his already busy schedule as a podiatrist. How did he work it out? He turned to the God who created him unto good works.

He told me, "Several years ago I prayed that God would allow me more time to do His work. It was only possible if my professional commitments could be simplified, specifically, if I were granted certain convenient hospital privileges and a surgical practice. God answered by opening the door for privileges at a local hospital, and by expanding my practice into the area of foot surgery. That meant less time in the office. God honored my desires and in turn enabled me to have more time to do personal ministry!"

HE PLANNED IT ALL BEFOREHAND

God prepared these good works "in advance," Paul says. This process was all sovereignly plotted out in eternity past. It involved a monumental planning and scheduling effort on God's part. Everything that will ever happen is part of His plan. He charted it out second-by-second for each life.

That's an amazing reality, but it's the great truth of our Christian faith. We don't have a God who says, "Go get 'em, son," and then leaves us to our wits to make it work. Nor do we have one who says, "I hope it turns out all right."

No, He planned out what would happen, as well as when and where. He made sure we would have the great opportunities that make life worth living!

In a way, God is like an architect who has blueprinted every step in building a house. However, not only has He planned what bricks will go into the facade, but also who will lay which ones, at what minute they will lay them, and who will hold the cement as the bricks are put into place. It's a four-dimensional blueprint that takes into account not only space but time.

This is a tremendous comfort to me as one who occasionally feels time-crunched. It means that if I can examine my life, rid myself of the temptations and diversions of "the evil days," there's a great chance that I will experience life as an adventure masterminded by the Master rather than as an annoyance controlled by the master deceiver.

THE ULTIMATE GOAL

What's the ultimate goal? That we might "walk" in those good works. God has not only designed the event, He's also made the appointment, got us dressed and coiffed, put us in the car, and guided us to the point of contact. Life is driving down Adventure Highway. At each juncture, He's scheduled opportunities for us to do good. We may have our own schedules. But the closer we walk with Him, the closer we'll come to seeing His work happen in our lives all day long.

So let the opportunities come. Our only job is to be ready when they're there.

ONE MORE THOUGHT

Yet one more thought. The fact that we are His workmanship means ultimately that we can relax and not be so hurried. Things will happen in God's good time. We don't always have to make it happen so much as be there when it happens.

We can also relax in the realization that He's very much in charge. Not doing all we planned to do is no failure.

David Ford, a teacher and professor in the Orthodox church, put it this way: "When I really start wondering whether I'm doing everything I should be, sometimes I'll pray that God will raise up someone else to do anything I don't get accomplished which I should have."

He added, "I hope that's not some kind of cop-out."

Frankly, it isn't. We're His workmanship. He, in the end, is also responsible. If we trust Him, we have every right to ask Him to take care of something we are unable to. We may play at being God. But He *is* God. He'd rather have us work at being His reverent and dependent children than play at anything else.

A tip on time: Take tomorrow and actively look for opportunities to do good—to offer an encouraging word, to tell someone how much you care and love him, to give a hand, to learn something new about life or the Lord, to offer a piece of advice from His word, to read an edifying thought. Pray that God will awaken you to the opportunities He's planned to come your way. Then open your eyes!

NOTES

1. Robert J. Samuelson, "Rediscovering the Ratrace," *Washington Post*, May 10, 1989.

2. Mark Porter, *The Time of Your Life* (Wheaton, Ill.: Victor, 1983), p. 16.

3. See *"poema,"* William F. Arndt and F. Wilbur Gingrich, *A Greek and English Lexicon of the New Testament* (Chicago: U. of Chicago Press, 1957), p. 689.

4. C. S. Lewis, quoted in *Leadership*, Winter 1989, p. 66.

11

Priorities Made in Heaven

The difference between the disorganized person and the calm, unflappable type is often that the second has determined what is important.
—Mark Porter, *The Time of Your Life*

A cathedral in Milan, Italy, features a remarkable entrance in which you pass through three doors in succession. Each door has an arch with an inscription. Over the first one, stone-etched and wreathed in roses, it says, "All which pleases is but for a moment." The second one pictures a cross with the engraving, "All which troubles is but for a moment." The climax comes with the third and largest doorway into the sanctuary. The inscription reads, "That only is important which is eternal."[1]

How do we plug into "that . . . which is eternal"? How do we begin to focus on what is important and stick with it?

J. Grant Howard offers a potent insight in his book *Balancing Life's Demands.* "We are surrounded by numerous options," he says. "Gathered around each of us is a massive array of alternatives. Some must be done, others can be put off. Some are bad. Others are good. Some tend to deceive us. Others try to motivate us. And the supply is ever-increasing—tending to overwhelm us. We are overstimulated, overchallenged, overexposed.

And if we don't watch out, we can become over-committed."[2]

So true. All our time-saving devices don't seem to be saving anything—time or dollars. Information doesn't come at us in words and phrases but in eight-hundred-page Congressional reports. The video store doesn't offer us a "few real heroes." No, one shelf might take us half a week just to skim the titles. The Christian bookstore features categories we didn't even know were categorized. The books, gadgets, devices, information, stuff, stuff, and more stuff run at us in tidal waves.

Nancy Gibbs writes in *Time*, "The computers are byting, the satellites spinning, the Cuisinarts whizzing, just as planned. Yet we are ever out of breath."[3]

How do you choose what to focus your eyes on, let alone decide to do or to buy?

The answer, says J. Grant Howard, is "PRIORI-TIES! The solution to our schizophrenic schedules is to establish the proper priorities. If we are going to get out of the rat race and live relaxed, normal lives, then we have to get our priorities straight."[4]

Yes, but what priorities?

THE QUESTION

What we need to ask is, What does God regard as priorities? We've looked at His goals. We've seen that He's capable, through His workmanship and sovereignty, to employ us in reaching those goals. But the goal is the target. Priorities relate to those actions necessary to accomplish the goals. It's often a choice between what is urgent and what is important.

Charles Hummel distinguishes between the "urgent" and the "important" in *Tyranny of the Urgent:* "We live in constant tension between the urgent and the important. The problem is that the important task rarely must be done today, or even this week. Extra hours of prayer and Bible study, a visit with that non-Christian friend, careful study of an important book: these projects can wait. But the urgent tasks call for instant action—endless demands pressure every hour and day."⁵

Mark Porter adds in *The Time of Your Life*, "The key to freedom lies in distinguishing between what's really important and what's merely urgent. . . . To choose between right and wrong is not difficult, but to choose between two good alternatives is not always easy. We can spend far too much time on some things, and far too little on others. The difference between the disorganized person and the calm, unflappable type is often that the second has determined what is important. He does not waste time, anxiety, or energy on the unimportant."⁶

That last sentence is key. Let me repeat it: "He does not waste time, anxiety, or energy on the unimportant."

Choosing between the important and unimportant is the key to time management and to life itself. I remember Howard Hendricks telling a class, "Gentlemen, the issue is not just choosing between what is good and what is bad; rather, it's choosing between what is good and what is better; and between what is better and what is best." Dr. Hendricks may have had a hundred opportunities for any given month, but he had to make selections among them. He had to decide what was important to him, and to his Lord, in order to make those decisions.

AN ANSWER

Yet, though many of the time management materials I've worked through are able to distinguish between what is urgent and what is important, they do not always look at what God deems important.

Years ago, there was much debate about "the order of priorities." Usually when asked, a student would put them in a sequential order: God first, family second, work third, church fourth.

What about the "self"? It was rarely discussed. It was almost as though we were embarrassed to mention the subject. Somehow making ourselves a priority was selfish, the flesh.

Yet, in reality we all put ourselves very high up on the priority list. Whose sandwich did we so carefully prepare and pack for lunch? Whose teeth did we brush? Whose car did we clean and shine with Turtle Wax on Saturday afternoon?

Shouldn't our priorities include "us"?

EVEN MORE TROUBLING

Then several years ago, someone gave me a little acronym that was supposed to help me make the right choices in life. It was J-O-Y: "Jesus first, Others second, You last."

Sounds really great! But when I thought about it, I realized, *That's impossible! It sounds pious, but it's ridiculous! No one could live up to that.*

What's the answer?

J. Grant Howard's analysis of priorities is eminently helpful. He sees priorities not as a sequence, but as a number of simultaneous responsibilities each of us has. He writes (italics added):

- God wants to be central in my life. This makes knowing Him a top priority. *He* is important.
- God wants to be significant in my life. This makes relating His truth to every aspect of my person a top priority. *I* am important.
- God wants me to know and do His will in each of the relationships that surround me. This makes my responsibilities in each of these areas (i.e., the world, family, work, government, and church) a top priority. *They* are all important.
- All these coexist as simultaneous responsibilities rather than sequential priorities.[7]

Doug Sherman and William Hendricks also offer some insight in *How to Balance Competing Time De-*

mands (Colorado Springs, Colo.: NavPress, 1989). They illustrate their concepts through the pentathlon sports competition in which an athlete is required to demonstrate excellence in five very different and difficult events—cross country running, a three-hundred meter swim, an equestrian steeplechase, pistol shooting, and fencing. Obviously, anyone who can master or even excel in these five areas goes far beyond the norm in athletic competition.

Sherman and Hendricks suggest that the Christian life, like the pentathlon, requires that we perform well in five very diverse areas: personal life, family life, work life, church life, and community life. The authors contend that walking with the Lord calls for a balanced and skilled performance in all those arenas, not just one or two.

The body of the book is an exposition of a personalized formula they call "A-P-P-L-Y," which refers to the steps we take in the process of balancing our lives.

A is for analyzing the Scriptures. *P* stands for taking personal inventory. The second *P* speaks of planning steps of action. *L* means making yourself vulnerable to others. And *Y* wraps it all up with yardsticks to measure your own progress.

The book is eminently helpful, especially to people struggling with integrating their working life with the four other elements of our Christian walk.

God Again

J. Grant Howard offers additional treatment of the subject that is supremely helpful. But again, I come back to the question, What does God consider important? Can we make it a little more concrete?

The problem is that no single passage of Scripture spells out a list of priorities. Paul's statements in Philippians 3 come close. Jesus' prayer in John 17 offers more insight into God's mind. But I think ultimately, we have to take the whole tenor of Scripture, seeking to boil it all down to a few clear issues about what God considers important.

Remember, God's goals are

manifesting His glory

establishing His kingdom

executing His plan

What, then, will be His priorities in accomplishing those ends?

I see at least five priorities in the life of Jesus, the teaching of Paul, and the rest of Scripture.

WORSHIP

John MacArthur calls worship "the ultimate priority" in his book by that name (Moody, 1983). The "great commandment" to love God with all your heart, soul, mind, and might is a call to worship. Jesus told the woman at the well that God seeks worshipers who will worship Him "in spirit and truth" (John 4:22-24). "The eyes of the Lord range throughout the earth to strengthen those whose hearts are fully committed to him" (2 Chronicles 16:9). He intends to support them.

Clearly, worship is a top priority item. But when we look at time in Mark Porter's chart in the previous chapter, only one-half year of a life of seventy-five years will be spent in worship and prayer.

But it doesn't have to be that way. It's possible to make nearly everything in life an act of worship—from playing softball to enjoying a New York strip steak to a pause on the subway to give thanks. If we take Paul's words in 1 Thessalonians 5:16-18 seriously, we will

rejoice always,

pray without ceasing,

and give thanks in everything

as a pattern of life. That is the essence of worship.

Obedience is a part of worship as well. Any way in which we're consciously obeying Him on the basis of

His Word qualifies as an act of worship. That ranges from doing a good job at work to your attitude as you put the dishes in the dishwasher.

In effect, given the right attitude and mind-set, we can worship God the whole day. Even sleep can be an act of worship as we "rest in the Lord."

Of course, all those hard-won habits of Bible memorization, Bible study, prayer, having a quiet time, special study, family worship, and so on, add minutes of our day to the living out of this priority. Knowing and learning of God becomes something we do as naturally as breathing.

I'm not trying to stretch it here. But the truth is that if worship is God's priority, it can be our priority too. It's a matter of attitude and effort.

DEVELOPMENT OF CHARACTER

The development of character relates to sanctification and the growth of holiness in our lives. As Paul told the Thessalonians, "it is God's will that you should be holy" (1 Thessalonians 4:3). God orders all the events of our lives to develop us in holiness and character. He gives us opportunities to serve and do good works. He puts us through trials and tribulations. It will all be designed to "[conform us] to the likeness of his Son" (Romans 8:29).

In the matter of time, our priority is submission to God's plan to make us holy. When we understand that He who "began a good work" in us is bringing it to completion in Christ (Philippians 1:6), we can relax. It's more important how we react and live than how much we make and do. Making a million dollars before the age of forty isn't the issue; how we use the ten we have is. Reaching the top of the ladder at our company matters little; but the integrity with which we conduct business cuts ice with God. Hurtling through the house doing the dusting, washing, vacuuming, and ironing in six hours flat doesn't touch heaven unless your heart "sang and made melody to the Lord" and you "gave thanks" in all things to the Lord (see Ephesians 5:19-20, KJV).

DISCIPLESHIP

Jesus' last command to the hundred and twenty was to "make disciples" (Matthew 28:19). Yet, how many Christians come even close to making one disciple in their lifetime, let alone disciples?

Yet, this is a top priority item in God's outlook. This priority includes all the other elements of preaching the word and leading people to Christ.

The time crunch in this area is astounding. Christians spend their time in the big splash: big socials, big seminars, big congregations, big Sunday school classes. But bigness clearly isn't better. Jesus did not spend most of His time with the five thousand men who were fed, or even the seventy-two who went out to evangelize. Rather, His priority was twelve men. Within the twelve, there were three—James, John, and Peter—into whom Jesus poured His life. But with those men, Jesus turned the world upside down.

If time management is the issue of "achieving maximum results in minimum time" as Ted Engstrom has said in *The Work Trap*, then discipleship exceeds the results. You get greater results by concentrating on less. You can make a lot of neat small holes with a shotgun. But one bullet from a "thirty aught-six" will stop a grizzly.

That also points up the truth of the old principle of doing God's will while leaving the results in His hands. A person who applies the priority of discipleship to his use of time may not see many immediate results. When Jesus died, ten of His disciples deserted Him. One had revealed himself a traitor and committed suicide afterwards. Only one other remained at the cross (John).

But God knows the end from the beginning. Any Christian who spends time in discipleship will certainly reap big rewards in the hereafter.

MEETING REAL NEEDS

At first "meeting real needs" sounds strange as a priority, but all it refers to is the priority of serving and loving your neighbor as yourself. Giving your attention to the real needs of what J. Grant Howard calls "your significant neighbors"—your family, church, immediate house neighbors, and co-workers—is important in God's eyes. This means helping people wherever they may be.

I say "real" needs, because there are many people who have needs that are simply desires, preferences, or demands. They're not genuinely matters of spiritual growth, personal health, and survival. Meeting real needs calls for the utmost in spiritual discernment.

One of the respondents to my questionnaire, who asked to remain anonymous, told me, "The area of ministry (study and people time) has always been a challenge for me in learning to avoid becoming overwhelmed. I am learning to block out specific time (on my calendar) each week for study and to make one, maybe two, dates to be with people in need or in relationship building. In the last six months one of these has been for 'hospice' volunteer work so I can be with the unsaved."

It just so happens that this same person found time to disciple me as a young long-hair hippie radical over seventeen years ago. The effects of her work are still with me.

But beyond discipleship, she was always a ready source of help, counsel, friendship, and love. I remember many times simply walking over to her house for a chat, breaking in on her day at any point. She always had time for me.

QUALITY OF WORK

Again, this priority didn't come to me easily. But I have recently been learning as a writer the value of qualitative versus quantitative work. Quality lasts. Often the things produced in quantity are out in a corner in the garage!

When God said, "It is good," after each of the seven creative days, He was commenting on quality. But don't let the word "good" deceive you. In our day, good "ain't so hot." But in Hebrew terminology, good was the penultimate achievement.

Our priority should be to do "good" works, to speak "good" words, to think "good" thoughts. Quality is paramount. Shoddiness is the easy route. Slipshod is simple. But to produce something that lasts and has true eternal value is a double achievement.

THE PRIORITIES GOD WANTS YOU TO HAVE

These five priorities can become a concrete guideline for us in the walk of everyday life. What are they again?

> Worship
> The development of character
> Discipleship
> Meeting of real needs
> Quality of work

Undoubtedly, there are others you might add to the list. But in order to

> manifest His glory
> establish His kingdom
> and execute His plan

these are the kinds of things we must give our lives to.

A tip on time: Think through your priorities. What things are important to you? Why are they important?

How do they compare to the divine priorities we've discussed? Are you in line with God's priorities, or out of sync? Why or why not?

Notes

1. Quoted in *Our Daily Bread*, December 1979.
2. J. Grant Howard, *Balancing Life's Demands* (Portland, Oreg.: Multnomah, 1983), p. 19.
3. Nancy Gibbs, "How America Has Run Out of Time," *Time*, April 24, 1989, p. 59.
4. Howard, p. 19.
5. Charles E. Hummel, *Tyranny of the Urgent* (Carol Stream, Ill.: InterVarsity, 1967), p. 5.
6. Mark Porter, *The Time of Your Life* (Wheaton, Ill.: Victor, 1983), p. 173.
7. Howard, p. 156. The italics have been added.

12

Redeeming the Time

You can participate in efficient meetings, and there-
fore make good tactical use of your time, but should
you have participated in the meeting in the first
place? Should the meeting even have been held?
That's when it becomes strategic.
                    —Don Guinn, Pacific Telesis Group

Dewey Gill wrote, "Days were plentiful and cheap
when I was young. Like penny candy, I always had a
pocketful—and spent them casually. Now my supply is
diminished, and their value has soared. Each one becomes worth its weight in the gold of dawn. Suddenly I
live in unaccustomed thrift, cherishing hours the way
lovers prize moments. Even at that, when the week is
ended, it seems I've gone through another fortune. A day
doesn't go as far as it used to."[1]

Gill's insight sets the biblical truth of "redeeming
the time" like a diamond against an ebony backdrop.
The idea is Paul's. It is found in Ephesians 5:15-17, a
passage we've already looked at several times. It bears
repeating: "Be very careful, then, how you live—not as
unwise but as wise, making the most of every opportunity, because the days are evil. Therefore do not be foolish, but understand what the Lord's will is."

The hurry, worry culture of modern America truly
is running out of time—ever since the day we were born.

We may not know how much we've got overall; but we definitely have less left than we did yesterday.

We must pay the price now and claim some of our present time for God's kingdom, or time itself will slip through our fingers without meaning, value, or accomplishment.

WHAT IS IT?

What is it to "redeem the time"?

Several images come to mind immediately. One is the age-old image of the mother telling her lazy son to "do something constructive with your time." "Constructive" isn't always defined, but it conjures up something worthwhile. It can be anything from making a drawing to building a skyscraper. But Mom wants to make sure you don't while away your day acting bored, complaining, snarfing snacks, and being a general nuisance.

PRODUCTIVITY

As we get older the maxim changes a little. Instead of "do something constructive," it becomes "do something productive." What is "productive"? Anything that brings in money, pays the bills, helps others, gets a needed job done, and the like. It doesn't have to generate an immediate reward like money, but it should "produce" something of value.

EFFICIENCY

Management and time experts sometimes liken the redemption of time to "efficiency." Get the job done with the least expenditure of energy and the maximum result. Charles M. Schwab, at one time president of Bethlehem Steel and one of the world's richest and most powerful industrialists, said, "Show me a way to get more things done. If it works, I'll pay anything within reason."[2]

The problem with this idea, though good, is that mere efficiency in production means little if what you produce is worthless. A factory could design and build machinery that produces the finest widgets possible with minimum energy and cost. But if no one wants the widgets, what use is the efficiency?

Similarly, a Christian might discover an incredibly efficient methodology for recording and editing preaching tapes. One instance I know of occurred at a church with a big tape ministry. They eliminated all the pastor's "pauses" on each tape so that the sermons ended up being shorter. Theoretically, the listener could get the same content faster. But the tapes were impossible to listen to and enjoy! What good is it if in the end no one wants to use it? Or worse, if God pronounces it a worthless pursuit?

CRAM IT FULL

Another way some people look at the "redeem the time" principle involves cramming every minute of life full of "eternally valuable" stuff. We're to "make the most of each hour." Thus, our day becomes jampacked with Bible reading, ministry, Bible memorization, prayer, witnessing, work, exhortation, encouragement, and other items regarded as valuable in the kingdom.

It's a nice concept, but it puts an incredible legalistic burden on each of us. We simply weren't created to "stuff" every minute full or to turn every hour of the day into a spiritual event. No normal human could ever do it. Even Jesus was accused of letting others waste time or of wasting it Himself (see Matthew 19:13-15; Luke 10:38-42).

EFFECTIVENESS

Still another element is Alan Lakein's "efficiency versus effectiveness" principle. He writes on the first page of his famous book on time management, "Please don't call me an efficiency expert. I'm an 'effectiveness expert.' Effectiveness means selecting the best task to do from all the possibilities available and then doing it in the best way. Making the right choices about how you'll use your time is more important than doing efficiently whatever job happens to be around."[3]

Again, this idea is excellent as far as it goes. The problem comes in the selection of jobs to be done. What is the best job and on what basis do you make the distinction? Lakein falls back on such things as your personal goals and priorities. But such an outlook is ultimately self-centered and self-aggrandizing. The Christian seeks to set his goals and priorities in line with God's plan and program, not his own.

Strategic and Tactical

Finally, people in the business world speak of strategic and tactical use of time. Don Guinn of Pacific Telesis Group tells in an article in *Fortune* magazine about the difference between the "tactical" and the "strategic." "Tactical time management," he says, "employs all the myriad techniques that help you get the most out of every hour." For instance, "You can participate in efficient meetings, and therefore make good tactical use of your time," says Guinn. "But should you have participated in the meeting in the first place? Should the meeting even have been held? That's when it becomes strategic."[4]

Guinn is expressing in different terms and with a slight twist ideas similar to those Alan Lakein and the others hold. He's seeing everything as part of his overall strategy in business and life. His strategy relates to how he will achieve his goals.

But again, we have to ask, what goals and strategies do you use? We've all seen the grand strategies of people on Wall Street like Michael Milken and Ivan Boesky, of people in the political realm like Gary Hart and Richard Nixon, and even of those in the religious

realm like Jim and Tammy Bakker. If your goals are out
of line with the ultimate goals of the kingdom, you may
win a battle or two. But ultimately, you'll not only lose
the war; you may lose your soul.

ALL THAT TO ASK

What is it to "redeem the time" in the scriptural
sense?

Paul's wording in Ephesians 5:15-17 is explicit.
Let's look closely at the terms. If we translate the passage literally, it could read, "Regard accurately how
you walk, not as unwise people, but as wise, buying the
time away from its master, because the days are evil."

Regard. The Greek word means to "see, observe,
watch."[5] In context it means to give attention to something, examine and study it closely with the purpose of
life change.

Paul is exhorting us to take a hard look at how we
live our lives. "Examine carefully how you walk and
live," he says. That calls for thought, discernment,
study.

Accuracy. "Careful precision."[6] That is, when you
look at how you're living, make sure you're getting an
accurate and truthful picture. Steer away from subjec-
tivity. Be as objective as you can. See your life as God
sees you.

Think of the process as a walk. "Be careful how you
walk." Paul is using the unique biblical term modern
Christians call our "spiritual walk with Christ." The
Christian life is like a long walk.

Stop and think about that a moment. A walk is relaxed. It's steady movement forward. It's easy, unhurried, firm, directed. It moves towards something far out
in front. It makes consistent progress. Ultimately, it gets
where it headed long ago.

As one who loves to walk as an exercise, I know the
simplicity and relaxation of a refreshing walk. There's
an ease about it that makes it fun and fulfilling to do.

I've tried jogging, nautilus programs, and exercise formats. But nothing beats walking. I never tire of it, and actually look forward to it every day.

Even when Paul spoke of us as "running our race," he never pictured the Christian life in the harried style we see today. The runner is disciplined, directed, determined. He runs in a relaxed, enjoyable fashion. He didn't mean the hundred-yard dash, but the marathon.

Thus, Paul is exhorting us to take a hard look at how we're wending our way through life. Are we making progress? Is it relaxing, restful, fun? Is it something you can wake up to with a sense of expectation and joy?

Wisdom. When Paul says "not as unwise but as wise," he's noting the importance of not only efficiency and effectiveness in doing tasks but the eternal value of what we're doing. Wisdom is from God. The wise person does a job right the first time. What he produces has genuine quality, both in the now and the forever. He's skilled in his use of time.

The unwise person rejects God's will, God's way, God's words. The wise person seeks God Himself, to know Him. He wants to apply His revelation to his life and circumstances. He sees life as ordered and orchestrated by God. Thus, he's not only able to make the most of time before the fact, but when the unexpected happens, he's ready to face it and act wisely in the midst of it.

Most important, he does not come at life like the executive who pictures himself as the author of an adventure he plans to fashion and manipulate to his own ends. No, he sees life as an adventure written by God in which he's a prime player. As the adventure unfolds, he relies on the Author to lead, strengthen, and guide him so that in the end he will not only triumph but will experience genuine fulfillment.

Redemption. The NIV and some other versions read "make the most of the opportunity." That's a fine idea, but I'm not convinced that was Paul's meaning.

The word Paul used meant to "buy something from someone ultimately to set it free."[7] It's the same word for "redeeming" us from the power of evil and placing us free in Christ's kingdom. So what does it mean to "redeem" the time? Think of a block of time as owned by an evil master. Within it you must do what the evil master dictates. He's already got a plan for what you will do in that period. Since that evil master has authority over you, you're helpless to resist.

But Christ has done something for the Christian. He bought him out from under the authority of that evil master. He made him His own and set him free. He's no longer under evil's authority. He neither has to listen to nor obey him.

However, there's one problem for us even though we're owned by Christ. The evil master still has a program and plan he wants us to obey. Thus, for any given block of time, he has ways of filling it with his foolishness.

Now we can come at the idea of "redeeming" that block of time. What we do is claim it and set it free to do those things that have eternal and righteous value, not evil. We come at a block of time, look at all the options available, and then, under Christ's authority, we claim that time for the kingdom.

THE TV HABIT

Here's a personal example. For several years my wife and I got locked into the habit of watching television from about 8:00 to 11:00 P.M. But one day we took a look at how we were living. We both decided that block of time was virtually owned by evil. So we redeemed it. We claimed that block for the kingdom and began doing in those three hours the things we believed had eternal value—Bible reading, family time, other reading, playing games, writing, listening to good music, and, at times, even watching decent television shows.

The amazing thing is that when we were caught in the TV watching habit, we constantly felt pressed for time and hurried—because we had to do the same work in three less hours a day. But when we "redeemed" that time, we suddenly felt more relaxed, unhurried, and in possession of a valuable block of time in which to get many good and important things done.

That's a fairly simple redemption of time, but it gets at the core of what "redeeming the time" is all about. It's claiming every block of time we can for the kingdom of God. It's not filling up the minutes with "productive" things. It's not just becoming more efficient or effective in our work, though those are elements. But it's actually hacking out an hour on the clock and putting a sign over it: "Do not disturb; kingdom work in progress."

Of course, your definition of "kingdom work" and mine might differ. We'll look at that in a later chapter. But the issue now is to begin hacking away at your twenty-four hours and begin claiming them for the kingdom.

Remember, though, you may be surprised at what kingdom time involves. It's not just Bible study, going to church, and so called "spiritual" pursuits. Rather, kingdom time can involve everything from getting dressed to a good night's rest. Everything in life can be kingdom time—if you'll take that hard look and begin staking those claims.

A tip on time: Examine the way you spent your day. What parts of it could be called "redeemed" time, and what parts clearly weren't? What steps can you take to keeping the same losses from happening tomorrow?

NOTES

1. Reprinted with permission from the May 1983 *Readers' Digest* [p. 238]. Copyright © 1983 by The Reader's Digest Assn., Inc.

2. Ted W. Engstrom and R. Alec MacKenzie, *Managing Your Time* (Grand Rapids, Mich.: Zondervan, 1967), p. 187.

3. Alan Lakein, *How to Get Control of Your Time and Your Life* (New York: Signet, 1973), p. 11.

4. Ford S. Worthy, "How CEOs Managing Their Time," *Fortune*, January 18, 1988, p. 88.

5. See "*blepo*," William F. Arndt and F. Wilbur Gingrich, *A Greek and English Lexicon of the New Testament* (Chicago: U. of Chicago Press, 1957), p. 32.

6. See "*akribos*," ibid.

7. See "*exagorazo*," ibid., p. 271.

13

Don't Worry, Be Joyful

When one has much to put into it, a day has a hundred pockets.

—Friedrich Nietzsche

A recent song carried the title "Don't worry, be happy." The singer assured us that there's nothing in life that should cause us to worry. Happiness is much more important. And being happy is what it's all about. So, don't worry, be happy.

The concept arouses something deep inside of us. We all want to reach that joyful plane where we no longer worry, we're happy. But actually, the Bible does not talk about happiness in the worldly sense of "feeling good and high on life." The Bible talks about being joyful, rejoicing, and finding happiness in God, His Son, His truth, and His coming kingdom. The reason we can stop worrying and start rejoicing is because of who God is, what He's doing, what He has done, and what He plans to do. Knowing Him and pleasing Him is all that really matters in life.

Yet, you might wonder if there's any way you can ever really please God. We come back to the old question: What does He expect of me anyway?

As I've read and studied the issues of time management, I feel a bit stifled. I have to ask: Is there any place for fun in the midst of all these priorities, goals, and time redemptions? After a while one feels as though life in God's eyes must be maximizing every minute for His kingdom with little room to jam in a laugh or a joke. Is it ever God's will to "waste" time? Or knock around in the shed? Or take a nap on a Sunday afternoon? Are these things verboten? Or at least, just lost time?

A quote from A. W. Tozer sheds some light on the matter. "Some of us are religiously jumpy and self-conscious because we know that God sees our every thought. We need not be. God is the sum of all patience and the essence of kindly good will. We please Him most, not by frantically trying to make ourselves good, but by throwing ourselves into His arms with all our imperfections, and believing that He understands everything and loves us still."[1]

God did not give us the Bible to burden us, but to set us free. He did not send His Son to portray a perfection we could never attain, but to show us what He wants to accomplish in us. He did not give us His commandments to pile on the guilt, but to help us live joyfully and fruitfully throughout our lives.

We Don't Believe It

Still, to some degree we don't believe it. So we fill up our time with things to do, places to see, people to meet. And somehow in the midst of all of it, we feel unfulfilled and unhappy.

Ellen Goodman, in a recent editorial titled "Teaching the Young to Hurry," laments her move from a vacation home in Maine to the pell-mell pace of hometown Boston, Massachusetts. She says, "With jars of wild blackberry jam wrapped carefully in T-shirts and towels, we are returning to the real world, although why we call it 'real' I cannot tell you. Is reality hard-edged and harried while fantasy is soft and leisurely? Is the real world one of obligations and the fantasy world one of pleasures?"

The real world is a world full of duty, impatience, sharp injunctions to "hurry up, hurry up," alarm bells, clocks, productivity, schedules, stress, pressure, and all those other "normal" things we live and move and have our being in.

She concludes: "Today, having just left the ocean for the city, I am most aware of the deliberate, even dutiful, way we prepare our children to lead the exact life we find so rushed. The pressure is on. Hurry, kids."[2]

WHAT'S IT ALL FOR?

But why? Why are we doing this to ourselves? What are we in such a hurry to do?

Have fun? Sure. At least, we're trying to. (Remember the bumper sticker "Are we having fun yet?")

Make lots of money? Definitely.

Plan for our future retirement? Of course.

Leave a legacy? That would be nice.

Make a mark for Jesus? That one's for us Christians.

But we're all trying so hard—so incredibly, almost ridiculously hard! Is this what Jesus meant when He said, "I have come that they may have life, and have it to the full" (John 10:10)?

This is life to the MAX?

Filled up—yes. But abundant?

GOOD OLD KING SOL

This is where King Solomon offers some stark and steady-eyed advice in the book of Ecclesiastes. He tried it all. He managed his time well and built palaces, temples, gardens, armies. He blew his time off in drunken parties and personal sex orgies with his many wives and concubines. He spent some time in study and concocted proverbs and wise sayings. He became the wisest of the wise and the richest of the rich, and he had more fun than anyone else while doing it. But he also decided that most of life was meaningless. He came to the place where he hated his own life.

Yet, several times in the course of the book, Solomon gives us a secret that we might miss if we speed-read it. Look at the following passages:

Ecclesiastes 2:24: "A man can do nothing better than to eat and drink and find satisfaction in his work. This too, I see, is from the hand of God."

Ecclesiastes 3:12-13: "I know that there is nothing better for men than to be happy and do good while they live. That every one may eat and drink, and find satisfaction in all his toil—this is the gift of God."

Ecclesiastes 3:22: "So I saw that there is nothing better for a man than to enjoy his work, because that is his lot. For who can bring him to see what will happen after him?"

Ecclesiastes 5:18: "Then I realized that it is good and proper for a man to eat and drink, and to find satisfaction in his toilsome labor under the sun during the few days of life God has given him—for this is his lot."

Ecclesiastes 11:9-10: "Be happy, young man, while you are young, and let your heart give you joy in the days of your youth. Follow the ways of your heart and whatever your eyes see, but know that for all these things God will bring you to judgment. So then, banish anxiety from your heart and cast off the troubles of your body, for youth and vigor are meaningless."

THE SECRET

What's the secret? *Simply to enjoy life as the good gift of God.* Isn't that incredible?

Solomon's conclusion is found in Ecclesiastes 12:13-14: "Now all has been heard; here is the conclusion of the matter: Fear God and keep his commandments, for this is the whole duty of man. For God will bring every deed into judgment, including every hidden thing, whether it is good or evil."

What does this have to do with time?

It means that creating goals, setting priorities, managing, hurrying, scurrying, scheduling, and achieving are all nice things to do. But if you don't enjoy what you're doing, or can't do it without inflicting yourself on others, what good is it?

How do you start to enjoy life anyway?

SOLOMON'S TOP SIXTEEN

Here is the meat of Solomon's advice as it applies to your use of time.

1. *Quit trying to figure everything out (Ecclesiastes 1:2, 3:11, 8:17).* You can't and you won't. Rather, trust God who understands it all as well as why it all happens the way it does.

David Ford, a professor of church history in Orthodox Seminary, told me about learning to trust God and be still in His presence. "I used to be quite anxious about whether I would get everything done that God had for me to do. But the longer I am in Orthodoxy—the longer I try to live by the accumulated wisdom of many saints through almost twenty centuries, the more a certain peace grows inside me, assuring me that as long as I'm trying to be faithful, and always asking His help and guidance, then whatever needs to get done will get done. The church Fathers and all the saints talk so much about stillness. 'Be still, and know that I am God'—Psalm 46:10—just abiding in Christ's presence, and nurturing this sense of peace which can then sustain and strengthen us as we do our necessary tasks."

It's an important insight. Robert Browning wrote:

> The lark's on the wing;
> The snail's on the thorn;
> God's in his heaven—
> All's right with the world![3]

That's trusting Him when we don't understand it all, or it at all. We realize we can't figure it all out, so why struggle at it day after day? Leave it in His hands.

2. *Quit trying to leave a lasting legacy (1:14)*. Whether it's making money, writing that bestseller, winning a top award, or building a monument to yourself, forget it. Only God knows what in human history will last from generation to generation. And what matters is what He thinks of it anyway.

Richard Baxter (1615-1691) understood this truth well. He knew what God had called him to and whether it lasted or not was not his concern. What mattered was doing God's will. Mark Porter writes that he was "a Puritan theologian, [who] published 128 books (more than 35 thousand printed pages) and was renowned for his house-to-house ministry in Kidderminster; yet he was a walking museum of pathological conditions. He wrote, 'I have these 40 years been sensible of the sin of losing time; I could not spare an hour.' He apologized for his books: 'I wrote them in a crowd of all my other employments, in the midst of continual languishing and medicine, which would allow me no great leisure for polishing and exactness, or any ornament.'"[4]

He didn't try to leave a legacy, just to minister in the here and now. He ended up ministering to the ages.

3. *Quit trying to learn so much (1:17-18; 12:12)*. Most of the information will depress you; much of it has no consequence. But above all, there's too much of it. You can't possibly absorb it all. Learn what you can, what you want, and what you need, and be satisfied with that. Don't compare yourself to others.

There's a story about Socrates that while he awaited death in prison, he heard a man sing a song by Stesichoros. Socrates asked the man to teach it to him. Knowing the great philosopher would soon die, the man asked why he wanted to learn something so difficult at such a late hour in life. Socrates replied, "I want to die knowing one more thing."

That's a good attitude. But the pursuit of knowledge, learning more, learning a bit here and there, can become an obsession. It's futile. You can't learn everything. Thomas Edison said in 1921, "We don't know the millionth part of one percent about anything. We don't know what water is. We don't know what light is. We don't know what gravitation is. We don't know what heat is. We have a lot of hypotheses about these things, but that is all."[5]

I read in *Campus Life* magazine that if you read twenty-four hours a day from age twenty-one to seventy and were able to retain all you read, you would remain one and a half million years behind when you finished!

Robert Frost said, "Piling up knowledge is as bad as piling up money. You have to begin sometime to kick around what you know."

Don't stop learning. But don't make it everything either. Keep it in balance.

4. *Don't take yourself too seriously, but take God very seriously (2:24-25; 5:1-5; 8:12; 12:1-8; 12:13).* Reverence Him. Honor Him. Fear Him openly. But by contrast, look in the mirror and have a good, long laugh.

Charles Hummel says, "Prayerful waiting on God is indispensable to effective service. Like the time-out in a football game, it enables us to catch our breath and fix new strategy. As we wait for direction the Lord frees us from the tyranny of the urgent. He shows us the truth about Himself, ourselves, and our tasks. He impresses on our minds the assignments He wants us to undertake."[6]

That's God. He's very significant.

On the other hand, what about you and me? Just how significant are we? A bishop noticed one of his disciples was very enamored with himself. So one day he told the lad to do something about it. He said, "Get yourself a jug full of water. Plunge your finger in, and then remove it. And the depression that is left is the measure of how significant you are!"

That's close enough for discomfort.

5. *Don't love things; they never satisfy (5:10).* You can never get enough. As John D. Rockefeller was asked, "What do you want?" He who had billions replied, "One more dollar."

A poem I cut out of "Radio Bible Class Digest" related these thoughts:

Take time to look: it is the price of success.
Take time to think: it is the source of power.
Take time to play: it is the secret of perennial youth.
Take time to read: it is the source of wisdom.
Take time to be friendly: it is the way to happiness.
Take time to laugh: it is the music of the soul.

And—above all—my own addition:

Take time to pray: it is the wellspring of
renewal, of hope, of life itself.

Time is not an opportunity to gather things; no, time is the stuff of life, the opportunity to live—for the Lord, for His kingdom, for loving and helping others.

6. *You can't always know what's best to do, so do what you want (6:12).* Sooner or later you simply have to choose among many good options. God is not going to write the answer in the sky, so choose on the basis of the facts, the truth, and *your personal desires!*

That's so startling, it throws many of us who have long been Christians. "What about God's will?" we cry. "What about doing God's work?"

That's paramount. But in many cases, God has given us a real choice, and He hasn't told us—either in principle, or in fact—what to do.

So what do you do? It's simple: Do what you want!

About a month after I became a Christian in the summer of 1972, I had to decide what I would do with my coming year since I might be going to medical school the next year. I sought the Lord's will about it, but it kept coming to me that I ought to do something I'd always wanted to do: spend a winter skiing in Vermont as a ski bum!

It struck me as incredible that God could want me to do this. But I listened to the inner promptings, and I decided to see if I could find a job that would allow me to ski. I went to Vermont, soon found a job, then stood outside in the cold air. I prayed, "Lord, do you really want me to do this?"

Of course, I got no verbal answer, but nothing within or without indicated I shouldn't. Finally, in frustration I said, "But Lord, that would be fun!"

Imagine, being able to do something "in" the Lord and having it be fun! It seemed incredible to me at the time, but now I see that much of the time God leads us to do the very things we already "want" to do.

7. *Enjoy things while you're doing them (2:24; 5:9; 8:15; 9:7).* Quit worrying about what's next. Start living it up now. Experience the present. If you're working, enjoy it. Get a kick out of it. If you're rolling on the floor with the kids, get into it. Stop grumbling about what you wish you could be doing! God's gifts to you are these very things in life—eating, drinking, playing, working. It's a gift. So make the most of it.

Bernard Berenson, who was an art historian, reveled in the joys of life. He lived fully. But as he neared the age of ninety, he remarked, "I would willingly stand at street corners, hat in hand, asking passersby to drop their unused minutes into it."

Take those "unused" minutes and enjoy them. *Now!*

8. *Find out what you like to do and do it (2:24; 3:22).* Do what matters and is significant to you. Stop worrying about the next guy. Enjoy your life while you have it.

Mark Porter writes of how John Calvin (1509-1564) worked towards his goals even against terrific odds and problems. He "produced the greatest literary work to come out of the Reformation, *The Institutes of the Christian Religion* (1536), while suffering from constant headaches, spitting of blood, a hemorrhoidal vein (the pain of which increased to unbearable proportions because of an internal abscess that would not heal), intermittent fever, gallstones, kidney stones, stomach cramps, intestinal influenza, and arthritis."[7]

John Calvin did something he loved and enjoyed, and he left a lasting mark. If what you have to do in terms of work and duty is no joy at all, why do it? Why not try to find a new way to fit in (without compromising truth) what yields genuine life?

9. *Try to include God in everything you do (2:24-25).* Whatever it is, recognize His presence and enjoy it.

Gordon MacDonald has come up with an interesting answer to the question of how Jesus managed to use His time so well. He writes, "All four gospel writers present to us a picture of Jesus under constant pressure, as He was pursued by friend and enemy alike. Every word of His was monitored, every action was analyzed, every gesture was commented upon. Essentially, Jesus had no private life to speak of.

"I have tried to imagine our Lord in today's world. Would He take long distance calls? Would He fly rather than walk? Would He be interested in direct mail campaigns? . . .

"Although His world was on a much smaller scale, it would appear that He lived with very much the same sort of intrusions and demands with which we are familiar. But one never gets the feeling when studying the life of Christ that He ever hurried, that He ever had to play 'catch up ball,' or that He was ever taken by surprise. Not only was He adept at handling His public time without an appointments secretary, He managed adequate amounts of time alone for the purpose of prayer and meditation, and for being with the few He had around Him for the purpose of discipleship."[8]

MacDonald goes on to point out three things about Jesus that helped Him be such an organized person.

1. He clearly understood His mission.
2. He understood His own limits.
3. He set time aside for the training of the twelve.

In other words, He included God's plan and work in everything He did. His life was a reflection of God's values, God's purposes, and God's plans.

10. *Do as much good as you can (3:13; 11:1-2).* A chance to do good is a gift from God, an opportunity. It even has a way of coming back to you. So keep those good deeds rolling on.

How do you start doing the most good you can? It's not very difficult to figure out.

Be open.

Be friendly.

Reach out.

Talk.

Touch.

Smell the roses.

Invite others to smell them with you.

Tell the Story to anyone who will listen.

Listen to everyone who wants to tell you their story.

Never turn down a child who wants you to give him a piggyback ride.

And never, never, never go sixty when you can get there punctually at fifty-five.

Above all, keep your eyes peeled and your ear to tracks.

Friedrich Nietzsche, no friend of Christ or faith, still hit an important nail when he said, "When one has much to put into it, a day has a hundred pockets."

11. *Don't take your own spirituality too seriously (7:16).* Hey, it's good to pray, read the Bible, memorize verses, and go to church. But you don't have to act all high and haughty about it! You might not only become a hypocrite, but also a flake!

I find that when I begin having my quiet time or going to church or teaching a class because I'm afraid God will zap me or refuse to bless me if I don't, I've begun to take myself and my spirituality far too seriously.

You're taking your spirituality too seriously when . . .

> you don't pray out loud with the group because you don't want to show them up,

> you feel that a visit was a waste if you didn't witness or leave a tract,

> you can't say, "I don't know the answer to that one," when you really don't,

> you get angry if anyone accuses you of not being "that" spiritual,

> you have to tell people regularly how many verses you've memorized, how much you read the Bible, or how much time you spend in prayer,

> you feel slighted if the pastor doesn't use you as an illustration,

Put yourself into any of those situations and see if the shoe fits.

12. *Don't let little things bother you (7:21-22), especially comments others make about you.* Forget the little insults, irritations, interruptions, jibes, cuts, and put-downs. It's not worth getting into a fight about it. Work toward peace—with everyone.

What is real peace? I once heard of a painting that pictured it. The scene was a monstrous ocean storm wracking the huge rocks along a beach. On first glance, it looked like anything but peace. But as you looked closer, you saw the point. There, in a depression in the middle of the rocks, nestled a bird—a sea gull or perhaps a pigeon or dove—on her eggs. Spray peppered the rocks about her. The wind howled. But that bird lay still, quiet, unafraid. Perfect peace.

She didn't have to fly out and flail away against the storm. No, she could be still and know that God was God.

13. *Try to stay out of trouble and conflict (8:5-6).* Who needs it? It kills off more time than anything. If you think some issue is a serious matter in the eyes of God, by all means jump into the fray. But otherwise, steer clear. What's the point of making an issue of something even Jesus would pass over?

It's interesting when you study Scripture the things that you find that Jesus didn't confront the disciples about. There's never any mention that He became upset about such things as wearing or not wearing a beard, length of hair, length of a woman's dress, drinking, joking, banter, overweightedness or underweightedness, the kind of music people listened to, entertainments, synagogue attendance, interruptions (especially people who just barged in and made their request), rudeness, or manners.

Not that these things aren't important. But how important? Important enough to start a personal war about it?

14. *Beware of all foolishness (10:1).* That's "sin" foolishness, anything that defies God's Word, law, or character. Avoid it like the plague.

Everywhere you look, there is sin. It'll do anything to get its hooks into us. Christians today often go far beyond simply flirting with the danger of sin; they walk right into it and declare it all right. The recent scandals involving Jim and Tammy Bakker and Jimmy Swaggart are stout testimony to that fact. Like Esau in the Bible, some have sold their lives, their ministries, and their character for a "bowl of stew." Their sin that in some cases lasted only a few minutes became the overpowering rule of their lives.

Flirting with sin is the utmost foolishness. Why? Because sin will never be satisfied with a flirt. It wants a full-fledged lover.

15. *Listen to your impulses and desires and respond to them (11:9-10).* Hey, some of those stray thoughts and ideas are good stuff—sent straight from heaven to you. If you don't grab them now, you'll forget them later. Just remember to weigh them against the truth.

I remember hearing Dr. Henry Brandt preach in my home church over a decade ago. He mentioned how he scheduled time "just to sit and stare." Time to think. Time to meditate. To let his mind rove over the possibilities.

16. *And one final word: remember that you will answer to God one day for everything you did in life (12:13).* So keep Him in a front row seat of your playing field.

"What was the secret of Jesus' work?" Charles Hummel asks in *Tyranny of the Urgent*. He answers: "Mark observes that 'in the morning, a great while before day, He rose and went out to a lonely place, and there He prayed' (Mark 1:35). Here is the secret of Jesus' life and work for God: He prayerfully waited for His Father's instructions and for the strength to follow them. Jesus had no divinely-drawn blueprint; He discerned the Father's will day by day in a life of prayer."[9]

Even Jesus knew He had to answer to His Father. Therefore, He sought His Father's will in everything so that when He did answer to Him, He would answer well.

A Gift

Not a bad list. I bet you didn't even know some of those statements were in there. I didn't! Solomon's point is that life is a good gift of God. The time you have, the days you live, the hours allotted to you *are a gift!* It's meant to bring pleasure not punishment, hope not horror.

So if you're hurrying about trying to accomplish this and that and something else over there, *stop!* Smell a just-matured rose. Read a paragraph of Wouk (or Michener, Perretti, Swindoll, or whomever). Sip a cool, tall one. Pluck a guitar string. *Stop* trying to make more of it than it is, and *start* making the most of what is!

In other words, enjoy the minutes as they come at you. You're only going this way once, so go for the gusto—with Jesus at your elbow, faith in your heart, and something gentle on your mind!

Ann Ruth Schabacker offers a fitting benediction,

> Each day comes bearing its gifts.
> Untie the ribbons.[10]

A tip on time: Are you hurrying more and enjoying it less? Maybe you need to sit back and relearn your childhood—the ability to wonder. Ask your wife or a close friend—"Am I too intense? Do I seem always in a rush?" Then ask them for their prayers and their help—to slow you down and experience God's good gift of life.

NOTES

1. A. W. Tozer, "A God Who Is Easy to Please," *Discipleship*, no. 47 (1988), p. 10.
2. Ellen Goodman, "Teaching the Young to Hurry," *Washington Post*, September 9, 1989, p. A15.
3. Robert Browning, "Pippa Passes."
4. Mark Porter, *The Time of Your Life* (Wheaton, Ill.: Victor, 1983).
5. Lehman Strauss, *Sense and Nonsense About Prayer* (Chicago: Moody, 1974), p. 122.
6. Charles E. Hummel, *Tyranny of the Urgent* (Carol Stream, Ill.: InterVarsity, 1967), p. 11.
7. Porter, p. 165.
8. Gordon MacDonald, *Ordering Your Private World* (Nashville: Thomas Nelson, 1984), pp. 74-75.
9 Hummel, p. 8.
10. Quoted in *Christian Science Monitor*.

Part 3

Choices:
Where the Battle Is Won or Lost

14

Your Kingdom or God's?

The kingdom of God is not a matter of eating and drinking, but of righteousness, peace and joy in the Holy Spirit.

—Romans 14:17

A member of a large church confided to me some personal frustration with his pastor. I asked him what was the problem. He blew away the smoke with these words: "He's building his own little kingdom."

In contrast, a reporter asked a well-known pastor if his goal was to "build a big church." He answered, "Not at all. Christ is building His church. I'm just investing my efforts in that church He's already building."

What a difference! Building your own little kingdom, or investing in the one Christ Himself is building.

THE BATTLE FOR YOUR TIME

The battle to control your time and invest in Christ's kingdom is one of the first choices each of us will make in our walk with Christ. Making the tough choices divides the soldiers from the civilians in the battle for your time. In this section, we'll look at a number of conscious choices each of us makes in the matter of time. One of the first ones we reckon with concerns Christ's kingdom.

THE FOOL

Building kingdoms is what Jesus' parable of the rich fool in Luke 12:16-21 is all about. The rich farmer was a fool because he invested his energies in a kingdom that would perish—his own farm, produce, and holdings. He laid up "things for himself" but was "not rich toward God."

It's in the same context that Jesus reiterated His timeless principle of seeking first God's kingdom. He said to His disciples in Luke 12:31, "But seek His kingdom, and these things will be given to you as well."

That statement raises an important question: What is it to "seek" God's kingdom?

THROUGH THE YEARS

Over the years I've heard a number of interpretations of that verse. One is that we are to "seek to establish" God's kingdom. We're to advance it, build it, invest our lives in making it a reality on earth.

The problem with that interpretation is that Jesus didn't include the word "establish." Jesus alone builds and establishes the kingdom—not us (see Matthew 16:18; 28:18-20).

Another interpretation is that we're to "seek the things of His kingdom and righteousness" in contrast to seeking the things of this world. That's considerably better. But I'm not certain it gets at the issue. Can Christ's kingdom be reduced to things?

If these ideas are not correct, then what is Jesus' meaning?

SEEK

The Greek word for "seek" carries several meanings. One is to look for and search out something, even to "obtain, strive for, or desire to possess" the kingdom.[1] This involves not only searching and looking but personal commitment. You want to take hold of it, make it yours, infuse your whole life with it.

A COMPARISON

I saw an analogy to this in the way we pursue things in this world. Recently, I purchased a cassette tape deck. In "seeking" to possess my tape deck I began a nearly devout pursuit of the best tape deck for the price. I went into numerous stores. I talked to sales people. I played special tapes and listened to the sound quality of the different decks. Finally, I settled on the type of deck I wanted.

But that was just the first step. Now I had to find the best price. (Believe me, this was pathological!) I cruised through malls and ducked into every store that sold stereos, looked to see if they sold that deck, and checked their price. I read the Sunday advertising section like a chocolate aficionado looking for the original cacao tree. I waited—months. I even prayed that God would help me find the best deal possible.

Then I hit it. I found the best price—anywhere in the universe! I plunked down my bucks and am now in possession of a fantastic tape deck.

The reverse of this is when I'm selling something. I also belong to a tape cassette club. Every now and then this club motivates us to get new members. If we get someone to sign up, I receive four tapes for free! (They get a good deal too—if you're interested, let me know!)

You can imagine my glee in this little charade. I began approaching all sorts of people—parents, relatives, fellow workers, neighbors—and even hooked a few. But to each I had to give a pitch. I played up the advantages. I told the truth about the disadvantages. I gave my personal testimony of how good this club is. I showed them the cost. I laid out the benefits. Then I left it in their hands. I became a virtual tape cassette club evangelist.

THE POINT, PLEASE

What's the point? Just this: the way I sought those material, earthly things is the way I should seek God's kingdom. How? With personal . . .

> effort,
>
> energy,
>
> expense,
>
> excellence of purpose,
>
> expectation of reward,
>
> exhilaration,

and all the while . . .

> entrusting the end to God.

When we seek God's kingdom, we pursue God's goals (His glory, kingdom, and plan) with His priorities (worship, personal character, discipleship, meeting of real needs, and quality).

THE KINGDOM

What is His kingdom? Through His disciples Christ reclaims places, people, and times in God's creation so that they all glorify and enjoy Him forever. We invade Satan's territory, marking it out as God's possession. "The kingdom of God is not a matter of talk but of power" (1 Corinthians 4:20). "The kingdom of God is not a matter of eating and drinking, but of righteousness, peace and joy in the Holy Spirit" (Romans 14:17). Christ's kingdom is "not of this world" (John 18:36). It "never comes by watching for it, . . . for the kingdom of God is within you" (Luke 17:20-21, Phillips*). In the new heavens and earth, God's "dwelling is with men, and He will live with them" (Revelation 21:3).

---

* *The New Testament in Modern English*, trans. J. B. Phillips (New York: Macmillan, 1958). Compare the NIV, NASB, and KJV, which use the phrase "by careful observation."

Ultimately, the kingdom of God is the present reign of Jesus. He calls people out of the evil world in order to make them citizens of the final and eternal kingdom of the future. When we seek His kingdom we fix our eyes and hearts on God in Jesus—all that He is, promises, and stands for—and commit ourselves to doing His will in our lives each day. It involves the seeking of His will (as revealed in His commandments) through His word and applying it in our lives.

How much of His word? All of it. Whatever part of it that relates to our present needs and circumstances. Whatever truths impinge on our relationships and responsibilities.

What Is God's Will?

Some people wonder, *What is God's will?* They're often seeking some specific statement from Him about what to do in their lies. There are a multitude of books available on knowing God's will for your life. Few, if any of them, have truly satisfied me. I've always come away feeling as though I had another huge load on my back— more rules, more principles, more conditions, more attitudes, more things to do.

Years ago, a co-teacher in my high school Sunday school class said something to me that etched itself permanently onto my soul. He pointed out that our group was in a high state of frustration about the Christian life. I asked him why.

"Well," he told me, "each week we go in there and give them two, three, or five principles about some passage of Scripture. Those principles are supposed to lead to life change. So we give them specific ways to apply the Bible to their lives. But if you add up all those principles in the course of a year, the end result is that you've given them two to three hundred things to do. That's getting close to the six hundred and some rules that the Pharisees established. And you know what Jesus said about them!"

I've thought about it for a long, long time. I'm convinced we preachers, writers, and leaders whom the brethren turn to in seeking to know what God expects must beware of becoming modern day Pharisees. We cannot, as Jesus said, "load people down with burdens they can hardly carry" (Luke 11:46). Piling up principles, processes, programs, and lists of guidelines for the Christian life is little more than the Pharisaical attempt to force everyone to keep the letter of the law.

AND YET . . .

And yet, what precisely does God expect of us? What is His will?

In a word, the Bible. The whole shootin' match. Every book, chapter, verse, clause, word, syllable, letter, and stroke! God's will is not only contained in the Bible. It's not part of the Bible. It's the whole thing. To paraphrase the title of a best-seller on the subject of sex, the Bible is everything God wants us to know about His will. So we don't have to be afraid to ask.

First John 5:3 sums it up rather precisely. "This is love for God: to obey his commands. And his commands are not burdensome." John is so strong on this subject that he says in 1 John 2:4: "The man who says, 'I know Him,' but does not do what He commands is a liar, and the truth is not in him." Not keeping God's commandments indicates we don't truly know Him.

WHOSE KINGDOM?

So whose kingdom will you invest your life in? Yours—in which your personal ambitions and desires take precedent—or His, in which His goals and priorities become your own?

Mark Porter offers a vivid illustration from the life of Clarence Darrow (1857-1938). One of the greatest criminal lawyers in American history, Darrow "was a master at manipulating juries, whether they were composed of homespun farmers or cultured aristocrats. He won freedom for the most hardened criminals. As a result, people were willing to pay huge sums for his services. He earned wealth, prestige, power."

But in his last years, unhappiness cut a hole in Darrow's heart. One day he heard a minister speak at the University of Chicago. Darrow asked for a personal meeting with him. Darrow told him, "I'm an old man, and I haven't found the way. Oh, in the eyes of the world, I'm a success. I chose criminal defense because I could make the most money and realize my potential. I had a way with men. I was so clever at it, I could get a fee of six figures for letting some rascal who was guilty go free. Now I'm old and wise enough to know that isn't life.

"I've been reading in the New Testament, and I came across a passage which is a fitting epitaph for my life. Jesus was preaching in the little boat by the seaside, and after His sermon, He told them to launch out and let down their nets for a great catch. The answer of one of those disciples is my life. 'Good teacher,' he said, 'we have toiled all night . . . and taken nothing.' That is Clarence Darrow, and if you have anything to tell an old man who has failed, say on, sir, because I haven't found the meaning of life."[2]

The choice you make—whose kingdom you will invest your life in—will affect your use of time every minute.

A tip on time: Take a few minutes now and evaluate. Are you consciously seeking God's kingdom, or are you hurriedly trying to build your own? Be absolutely honest with yourself and God. Afterward, take a moment and pray, confessing your pride, ambition, and self-reliance, and ask God to redirect you creatively and fruitfully.

NOTES

1. See *"zeteo,"* William F. Arndt and F. Wilbur Gingrich, *A Greek and English Lexicon of the New Testament* (Chicago: U. of Chicago Press, 1957), p. 339.
2. Mark Porter, *The Time of Your Life* (Wheaton, Ill.: Victor, 1983), pp. 14-15.

15

Vacillating Interest
or Valued Intimacy?

*I guard my time with the Lord. Busyness is the biggest
hindrance to genuine spirituality.*
—Jim Dethmer, pastor,
Grace Fellowship,
Baltimore, Maryland

On the first page of his famous book *Power Through
Prayer*, E. M. Bounds writes, "We are constantly on
a stretch, if not on a strain, to devise new methods, new
plans, new organizations to advance the Church and se-
cure enlargement and efficiency for the gospel. This
trend of the day has a tendency to lose sight of the man
or sink the man in the plan or organization. God's plan
is to make much of the man, far more of him than of
anything else. Men are God's method. The Church is
looking for better methods; God is looking for better
men."[1]

Bounds begins that very chapter with a quote from
Robert Murray McCheyne, the nineteenth-century Scot-
tish pastor who lived only thirty years but influenced
millions. McCheyne wrote, "Give yourself to prayer,
and get your texts, your thoughts, your words from God.
Luther spent his best three hours in prayer."

A Startling Statistic

In contrast to those words, my pastor revealed this startling statistic in a recent sermon: "The average evangelical pastor spends five minutes a day in prayer."

If our leaders are only spending five minutes, what of the average layman? Yet, it's prayer and intimacy with God which is the highest priority of life. Jesus told the devil, "Man does not live on bread alone, but on every word that comes from the mouth of God" (Matthew 4:4).

Is the time crunch a reality or simply the consequence of failing to love and worship God on a daily basis? For it's through relating to God in that way that we discover . . .

the will of God for our lives and days,

the power of God for service,

the comfort of God in suffering and worry,

the encouragement of God for endurance,

the cleansing of God for true freedom,

the wisdom of God for solving our problems,

the rest of God for true peace,

the contentment of God for divine satisfaction in life,

the life of God for final fulfillment.

Ask yourself: are these things important to me? Is this what I yearn for and desire in life?

Then intimacy with God must become a scheduled priority. It's that simple.

People Say . . .

People have repeatedly told me as I did research for this book that scheduling and keeping personal time with God is the number one priority for order and joy in their use of time.

It can take many forms. Some people carry on devotions in the early morning. Others find that quiet spot at night just before bed. Others at lunchtime, or on their coffee break, or after dinner. Some spend five minutes, others five hours. But whether it's five minutes or five hours, it's a date the Christian must learn to keep.

The processes are different, too. Some follow a rigorous pattern of fifteen minutes in Bible study, fifteen minutes in Bible memorization, and fifteen minutes in prayer. Others use devotional literature or a special book. Still others write in a journal, or meditate on a word like *love* or *holiness* throughout the day. I even remember a friend in seminary who read Robertson's huge *Greek Grammar of the New Testament* for his QT!

What matters is that your time with God fits you, your needs, and your life situation. My experience is that the Lord works in us in different ways at different times. As we grow, we'll see our methodologies change dramatically over the years.

The point is that we schedule that time, and keep it.

THE DISORGANIZED CHRISTIAN

Gordon MacDonald writes in *Ordering Your Private World* that "disorganized Christians rarely enjoy intimacy with God. They certainly have intentions of pursuing that camaraderie, but it never quite gets established. No one has to tell them that time must be set aside for the purpose of Bible study and reflection, for intercession, for worship. They know all of that. They simply are not doing it. They excuse themselves, saying there is no time, but within their private worlds they know it is more a matter of organization and personal will than anything else."[2]

Which comes first, getting organized or intimacy with God? The answer is simply to get organized enough to have intimacy with God and God will help you get organized!

Jim Dethmer, pastor of Grace Fellowship in Baltimore, Maryland, a church that has grown to over a thousand members in a few years, told me, "I guard my time with the Lord. Busyness is the biggest hindrance to genuine spirituality."

Lance Quinn, a manager with Grace Communications in California, asserted, "Spend time faithfully with God and His word. That will take you away from the tyranny of the urgent."

Pat Buysse, a wife, mother, and writer in Derwood, Maryland, offered, "I have found that for years I put my time with God first out of duty and sometimes guilt. But now, through habit it has become a special time I want and need. I can't go on very well without putting Him first."

How Did Martin Luther Do It?

Martin Luther was quoted earlier as saying, "I have so much to do today, I'll have to spend the first three hours in prayer or the devil will get the victory." Martin Luther is the most written about man in world history next to Jesus Himself. His personal translation of the Bible into German is still a standard today. He wrote commentaries on the whole Bible, as well as numerous other books. He pastored churches and was the lighthouse of the Protestant Reformation. How on earth did he do it?

Luther left us an answer. He explained his devotional habits in a letter to his barber. It was published under the title "A Simple Way to Pray, for a Good Friend." Walter Trobisch interprets the letter in his book *Martin Luther's Quiet Time*. What, then, did Luther do?

It's nothing extraordinary. He included both Bible study and prayer and urged that we meditate on the Scriptures. But as we do so, we should ask questions. He also recommended that we use a notebook to write whatever meditations and thoughts occur to us. First,

Luther says to ask, *What am I grateful for?* We ask this question specifically of the text we're meditating on. What "in" the text am I grateful for? Take a text like "God is love." What might we be grateful for from that? That God loves us, yes. But let's go deeper. That God is love means everything—and I mean everything—that happens comes from a heart of love. So I can be grateful for all that happens, knowing that it comes from His heart of love.

That God is love also means the essence of His being is love—thinking, feeling, and acting in a loving way. He can never do anything other than love me wholly and infinitely. I can be grateful for that love, feel its warm security, and rejoice that this God is my personal friend.

Meditate on that a moment. What thanks can you give Him because of it?

Second, as we meditate on the same text, ask, *What do I regret, or what makes me sad?* This leads to confession of sin.

To take the same text, I remember that I am to be like my Father in heaven. How have I not been loving? To whom have I not been loving? What can I do to make it up?

Third, ask, *What in the text leads me to intercession for myself or others?* Is there something there I need to pray about? Does the fact that "God is love" lead me to ask to become more loving? To whom? How? What can I do?

Finally, *What am I to do?* That calls for a personal, specific application of the Scripture to your life. This gets down to the nitty-gritty. To whom will I show love today? When? Where? How?

You can do this with any text. In that three hours, Luther would actually plan his day as he talked with God and meditated on his word. When distracting thoughts entered his mind, he would turn them into reasons to pray and include them in his devotions.

It was in this time that Luther actually plotted out his work, hand in hand with God. That was why he could spend the first three hours in prayer—because he talked with God about everything he wanted to do that day. It's an old principle: more time in planning leads to less time in execution. When your co-planner is God Himself, how can you fail?

CRUNCHING THE TIME CRUNCH

Linda Rapp, a pastor's wife and professor at Biola University, related to me a fascinating experience with these truths.

She wrote me, "The real breakthrough in my addiction to busyness came a couple of years ago in the spring of 1986. I was carrying a full doctoral course load at UCLA and teaching English at Biola, where I also coordinated placement testing, tutoring, and curriculum for the Non-Native Speaker courses there. [Linda is of Chinese descent, and speaks fluent Chinese.] I was also revising a methodology curriculum for a summer teaching training program overseas. Plus, I was active in both the children's and music ministries at our church where my husband is pastor."

Whew! I'm tired just writing it. But she goes on, "As various deadlines closed in on me, I found myself really pushing my limits—climaxing in a string of six all-nighters in nine days. Not only was I physically frazzled, but I also was struggling with my attitude toward the projects and commitments." Linda was not only at the end of her rope, but literally hung out awaiting burial! But she says, "God used two passages to speak to me during this time: Romans 5:1-5 and Joshua 9."

Through Romans, she says, "I was reminded that in God's gracious provision of peace with Himself I always have a reason to rejoice and a reason to hope. These truths gave me motivation to persevere, and protected me from burnout."

But the second passage reminded her of "how Joshua and the Israelites compromised themselves by foolishly getting drawn into an undesirable treaty with the Gibeonites. They 'did not inquire of the Lord' (Joshua 9:14). Their mistake could have been avoided if only they had taken time to pray about their decision first."

Linda was convicted. She asked herself, "Of the sea of commitments I had been drowning in, how many would I still be involved in if I had conscientiously inquired of the Lord before saying 'yes'?"

She concluded, "Prayer is the best busyness-buster I know!"

I don't think I need to add anything to that!

A **tip on time:** Evaluate your devotional life. Are you drawing closer to God, or away from Him? Would you be embarrassed to tell your pastor about how much time you spend in prayer and seeking God? If so, what can you begin doing now so that you might share the truth with joy?

NOTES

1. E. M. Bounds, *Power Through Prayer* (Grand Rapids, Mich.: Zondervan, 1962), p. 11.
2. Gordon MacDonald, *Ordering Your Private World* (Nashville: Thomas Nelson, 1984), p. 72.

16

Things on Earth or Treasure in Heaven?

Do not store up for yourselves treasures on earth, where moth and rust destroy, and where thieves break in and steal. But store up for yourselves treasures in heaven.

—Matthew 6:19-20

The problem of things and time was brought home to me in a fresh way by Eileen Merrell. She told me, "For most of our marriage, Mike [her husband] has worked two, sometimes three jobs. He was burned out. So I picked up the extra job. Then I felt I was slighting the kids."

The problem, though, was money. Too many debts. Not enough time to make up the slack.

She went on, "We needed to learn to pray before every purchase. Do we really need it? How will we pay for it? Whose time will be sacrificed? We found that the old saying, 'time is money,' should be reversed. 'Money is time.' If we need to pay, we need to work for the money. Thus, the time crunch."

We can see the time crunch hanging hard and heavy over all of us in this area. Things not only crowd our lives; they cause us to make poor, covetous decisions that lead us into a tighter vice of worry. If Satan can hook you with the latest gadget, he'll also claim

more of the time you'll need to spend making the money
to pay for it!

MATERIALISM

The materialism of our age is nearly astonishing,
and it's a prime cause of our time crunch. We work longer hours in order to make more money so we can buy
more.

A recent survey of freshman college students has
discovered that they're experiencing more "anxiety
over long-term financial prospects."[1] In other words,
they're worried they won't make enough money when
they get out of college.

Another article revealed, as I reported earlier, "The
good life, the Census Bureau reported yesterday, is
founded now on two paychecks. Overall, according to
the study, about 26 million of the nation's 89.5 million
households, or 29 percent, had enough left over for luxu-
ries after payment of all basic costs to provide a comfortable style of life. . . . The average before-tax income
of the 26 million households was $56,605."[2]

$56,605! That's what you need today to "live the
good life." In a more humorous vein, an article in *The
Washington Post Magazine* illustrated the situation:
"Let's pause for a moment to bemoan the fate of yuppies. Those poor spoiled brats have fallen not only from
favor but also, apparently, from the heights of purchas-
ing power. . . .

"About a year ago, came the three tsunamis that
washed over these hapless pioneers of conspicuous con-
sumption. First were the changes in tax laws, which
limited business write-offs for expensive cars and gradually eliminated the tax deduction for interest pay-
ments on car loans. Then Wall Street caved in. . . That
set up the final wave: increases in the costs of European
cars approaching 30 percent. Yuppies are borrowers,
but enough is enough."[3]

Is it worth it? Is that what we're going for?

THE ANSWER

What's the answer? "Do not store up for yourselves treasures on earth, where moth and rust destroy, and where thieves break in and steal. But store up for yourselves treasures in heaven" (Matthew 6:19-20). It's being "rich toward God" that counts and lasts (Luke 12:21).

How do you become rich toward God? Jesus specifically answers the question in Luke 12:33: "Sell your possessions and give to the poor. Provide purses for yourselves that will not wear out, a treasure in heaven that will not be exhausted."

A multitude of other Scriptures indicate that Jesus wasn't against having things, or even saving money. But the primary reason some have money and others do not is so that the ones who have can help the ones who have not (see 2 Corinthians 8-9). Hoarding the things of this world, hedging against an uncertain future is the ultimate foolishness. So is the continual buying of stuff!

Ask yourself how much the quest for things controls your time. What things are you now working to purchase (or paying off, which is more likely), which causes you to scramble, scritch, and scratch ten to twenty extra hours a week in overtime work? Maybe you need to reevaluate.

CHANGES IN LIFE-STYLE

One Christian who has faced the reality of things on earth versus treasure in heaven is Bill Tamulonis, from Baltimore, Maryland. He's a member of Grace Fellowship, a fast-growing church in Baltimore that helps people in the hurried life-style. Bill works in marketing at Maryland National Bank. He told me, "I started thinking about the most important things in life, what I wanted to give my life to. I discussed it with Jim [his pastor—Jim Dethmer]. He challenged me to go for it spiritually, to get into some kind of worthwhile ministry.

"I decided I wanted to get some training. So I'm now in the Master's program at Capitol Theological Seminary in Washington, D.C. I also wanted to be more involved in local church ministry. We'd also just had a baby. But I knew I couldn't do everything. So I began seeking an alternative work schedule, something more flexible."

What did he do?

"Maryland National was developing a program of a four-day week—four nine-and-a-half hour days, Monday to Thursday. I decided to try it."

How has it worked out?

"Wonderfully. I've been at it about a year. There's been improvement in all areas. I feel more fulfilled and able to do what I want to be doing. Furthermore, it hasn't hurt me career-wise. I even received a promotion since I've taken this new job. I know they'll let me make career decisions. I'm not locked out of consideration for advancement."

STARTING YOUR OWN BUSINESS

Another member of Grace Fellowship, Rich Tucker, decided to start his own business to get out of the time/career crunch. He explained, "I was very involved in my work, progressing in the company. More and more hours. Seventy hours a week. A lot of travel. I wasn't meeting my family needs or my work needs. And I could see my nine-year-old son was hurting.

"So I started my own company with three partners eighteen months ago. Electronic equipment and Radon testing. All four of us are family-oriented men. Our hope is that we can develop the business, keep it small and profitable—enough to meet our financial needs and still pursue other interests—like going to Bible school. I'm able now to do the things I want to do."

Tom Kosnik, until recently a professor at Harvard Business School, was interviewed in an article appearing in the *Wall Street Journal.* The thirty-eight-year-old professor had been working a "frenzied" seventy-five hours a week. No more. "Now he and his wife are moving to northern California, a region they love, because 'we need more time for fun—for travel, physical fitness, friendships, and spiritual reflection.'" He has opted for a slower-paced career as a consultant and writer.

NOT JUST WORK EITHER

Still, these attitudes carry over into other areas, not just career or work. Howard Hendricks wrote me, "Early on I committed myself to the goal that even if I was never known as a great writer, speaker, or seminary professor, I wanted to be known as an adequate father and husband. People can always be ministered to by others perhaps more effectively, but I am my wife's only husband, my children's only father. 1 Timothy 3:4-5 [characteristics of an elder—a good manager of his home] speaks volumes to me. I find it possible to be eminently successful professionally and a total failure parentally and maritally."

Someone once told me the way to store up treasure in heaven is to invest in something going to heaven. That's your family, your church, yourself, the people around you. Invest it in what lasts forever, and you will have a happy forever!

Henry Wadsworth Longfellow wrote:

> Trust no future, howe'er pleasant!
> Let the dead past bury its dead!
> Act—act in the living Present!
> Heart within and God o'erhead.

A **tip on time:** What are you investing your life in? Take inventory. How are you spending your money? Is there anything close to a tithe (10 percent)? Or is your life crowded with things you have and things you still want? Ask yourself the hard questions, and answer them before God. Then think about how you're living and what changes you might make. Write them down.

NOTES

1. Barbara Vobejda, "Freshmen Reporting More Stress," *Washington Post*, January 9, 1989, p. A18.
2. Spencer Rich, "Prescription for the Good Life: 1 Household, 1 Paycheck," *Washington Post*, May 25, 1989, p. A9.
3. Brock Yates, "How Much Is That BMW in the Window?" *Washington Post Magazine*, December 18, 1988, p. 39.
4. Carol Hymowitz, "Stepping Off the Fast Track," *Wall Street Journal*, June 13, 1989, p . B1.

17

Playing Around
or Plowing Forward?

*On my calendar there are but two days: today and
That Day.*

—Martin Luther

Doug White delivers packages for UPS. One day on
the road he witnessed a traffic accident. "It really
changed my outlook," he said. He's been a Christian for
over six years. "I realized that each day could be my
last. I have to weigh that against how I'm doing with my
family—my son and wife, who are my first and most important disciples. I began to ask myself, 'Did you enjoy
your son while you had the time?'"

Dave Kruegar, on staff with Search Ministries, a
life-style evangelism ministry based in Lutherville,
Maryland, had a similar experience. "My father had
died suddenly. I went to his house and, in the process of
going through his things, I went down into the base-
ment. My father was a hunter. He had shotguns and ri-
fles, and he used to reload his own shells. I wasn't upset
or anything, just looking through them. I found a shell
he'd reloaded, as well as some empty ones. It was then
that God spoke to me. The thought came into my mind
that every decision I make had to be a live round and
not an empty casing."

Kruegar had to ask some hard questions. "What is God's purpose for me? Why am I doing what I'm doing?" He said, "We have to ask those questions constantly. It's not a tension we ever ultimately resolve."

OBSESSED WITH TIME

It's easy to become obsessed with time. Any moment may be your last. You've got to make it count! But at the same time, you can't do everything. Getting hung up in that desperate hurry to get everything done NOW can become neurotic.

An article in the *Wall Street Journal* pointed out that many young businessmen building their own businesses often get hung up on their use of time. One person interviewed, Jon Hirschtick, chairman of Premise, Inc., a Cambridge, Massachusetts, computer software company, said, "If I watch TV, I want to watch four channels at once, switching around. If I have three hours free on Sunday morning, I want to get a lot of things done. I can't sleep as long as I used to." He tends to work seventy to eighty hours a week.[1]

NOT GOD'S WAY

But did God create time for us to become obsessive maniacs bent on cramming our schedules so full we eventually explode? I think not. How do we avoid that trap?

The long view. Looking down life's narrow way and envisioning a destination we want to reach. Martin Luther said, "On my calendar there are but two days: today and That Day." "That Day" has a direct bearing on today. Unless we've taken the "long view" and scrutinized the reality of That Day—judgment and the Bema of Christ—we'll never get under the Spirit's charge and live in His power. He can only direct a moving object. But He can only take it somewhere if there is somewhere to go to.

I believe this is Jesus' thought in Luke 9:62: "No one who puts his hand to the plow and looks back is fit for service in the kingdom of God."

It's an excellent snapshot of time in the kingdom of God. Life is like a man guiding a plow through a field. How well he controls and guides that plow depends on his expertise and experience as a farmer. But making a straight furrow—using your life to please God—takes something more. What? This: having a goal, a destination, a target at which you're aiming. Without goals, we're little more than castaways wading through a swamp with no hope of finding home. But goals can motivate and energize.

THE PLOWMAN

In order to make a straight furrow in his field, a plowman needs several aids. In these thoughts we see some important principles about setting and using goals in our lives.

1. *A clear target.* He fixes his eyes on some object, or target, at the end of the furrow, then moves toward it, guiding the plow behind the ox or mule. If he looks down or back, he'll inevitably contort and twist himself and ruin the straightness of the furrow. Straight furrows make for a tidy, more productive field. So straightness is paramount. A target to move toward helps.

2. *Concentration.* To cut a straight furrow, that plowman must concentrate on his work. He fixes that point far down at the end of the field in his mind and pushes towards that point. He's single-minded, not looking around, not looking back, not musing on some other subject. He's fully concentrated. Every muscle moves in response to his purpose. His mind doesn't wander. He's not daydreaming. He's moving toward his goal with precision and passion. He will not waver.

3. *Control.* A plowman also needs control. Steadiness. A firm hand on the plow. As he plows, he has to take care of that horsefly on his shoulder, that rock in

his path, his mule's penchant for stopping and refusing to move, and his own discouragement—and all without losing sight of his goal. He must learn to be in charge while being flexible.

4. *Perseverance.* Above all, a plowman must stick with the task and see it through. Paul expressed this idea in 2 Timothy 4:7: "I have fought the good fight, I have finished the race, I have kept the faith."

He hung in there. He gave it his all. He stayed with the program. He never threw in the towel.

5. *A measurable distance.* The plowman doesn't plow from Canada to Mexico. No, it's a short, measurable, realizable distance. It's long enough to require faith, but short enough for him to believe that he can do it with God's help.

6. *A reward.* When he reaches his target, as he turns around to do another row, he has a reward: one straight furrow finished. For a moment he can celebrate, give thanks, and rejoice. Then he can move on.

PLOWING A STRAIGHT FURROW

Despite all the stresses and pressures of modern-day living, there is a way to plow a straight furrow. Have a clear target, concentrate, stay in control, persevere, go a measurable distance, and look back. Presto! You've accomplished something!

That is what goals are all about for us as Christians. Having goals helps us set the priorities that ultimately enable us to govern our time under the Spirit's power.

Dr. Ari Kiev of the Cornell Medical Center has written, "Observing the lives of people who have mastered adversity, I have repeatedly noted that they have established goals and, irrespective of obstacles, have sought with all their effort to achieve them. From the moment they've fixed an objective in their minds and decided to concentrate all their energies on a specific goal, they began to surmount the most difficult odds."[2]

PERSONAL GOALS

I remember a goal-oriented professor in seminary exhorted us to write down our goals and refer to them daily. At that time it was an intriguing idea. But I didn't follow through.

Years later, and with a little more maturity under my scalp, I began to see the beauty and power of just such a process. I wrote down a list of goals—things I wanted to accomplish in my life on earth—and put them in my wallet. Every now and then I pull them out and read through them, then offer up a word of prayer. Occasionally, I discover I've reached a goal. That's a reason for praise. On other occasions, I realize that what was once an important goal is no longer; I lay it aside. And in other cases, I find my initial goal was too small. So I rewrite it and make it bigger.

Keeping these goals in my wallet keeps them in my consciousness. I'm always thinking about them, how to reach them, what I need to do today to move in that direction.

YOUR GOALS OR . . . ?

But if you merely pile up a list of personal goals that have no bearing on God and His kingdom, you're making a mistake. That's like winning the battle but losing the war.

As we discussed in the chapter on God's goals, taking the long view means to consider His plans for the world as revealed in Scripture, and then submit our own goals and plans to them. Proverbs speaks of the process.

"Commit to the Lord whatever you do, and your plans will succeed" (Prov. 16:3).

Someone said, "The chief purpose of life is to invest in something that will outlast life." That's the process of choosing goals for your life that are embedded in God's plan and program. When we subject our plans to the

Lord's plan, we're guaranteed that we'll reach them. God Himself is committed to it!

WORKING IT OUT

Working through your goals frees you to do what is important, not just what's there. Thinking through your goals—and you must if you want to eliminate hurry from your life—is not difficult. Simply get a crisp, new sheet of paper and write out where you want to be in ten years, or twenty, or thirty. What do you want the Lord to reward you for at the Bema Seat? Make them specific. Make them measurable (that is, concrete enough so you can see when they've been reached). Make them possible—but only through faith. That is, they should be small enough that you believe you can reach them, and big enough so that you know you can only reach them if God helps!

Consider all areas too: personal life, work, church, community, family. Develop goals under each heading. Then keep them in your wallet or pocketbook. Refer to them daily. Pray through them. Change them as need arises.

INCORPORATING GOALS INTO YOUR DAILY LIFE

How, then, can you incorporate your goals into the everyday flow and ebb of daily life? Let me offer you several thoughts:

1. *Plan well in advance.* Use a calendar. Incorporate your goals into the calendar.

In *Ordering Your Private World* Gordon MacDonald writes, "I have learned the hard way that the principal elements of my time budget have to be in the calendar eight weeks in advance of the date." Eight weeks!

"What goes into my calendar? Those nonnegotiable aspects of my private world: my spiritual disciplines, my mental disciplines, my Sabbath rest, and of course my commitments to family and special friendships.

Then a second tier of priorities will enter the calendar: the schedule of the main work to which I am committed: sermon study, writing, leadership development, and discipling.

"As much as possible all of this is placed in the calendar many, many weeks in advance of the target week, because as I get closer to that week I discover that people move in to make demands upon the available time. Some of them will have legitimate demands, and it is to be hoped there will be space for them.

"But others will have demands that are not appropriate. They will request an evening that I have scheduled for the family. Or they will want an hour in the morning reserved for study. How much better my private world is when I allow that work to flow around the priorities and into available slots than when things are the other way around."[3]

When people simply barge in and request your time, you can always pull out your calendar and tell them, "I'm sorry, I've scheduled something at that time." Usually, they'll bow out or ask for another slot.

2. *Find your own pace. Take a goal in small bites.* The author John Erskine noted that at the age of fourteen he learned a valuable lesson from his piano teacher. He told his teacher he practiced for an hour or more at a time. The teacher answered, "Don't do that. When you grow up, time won't come in long stretches. Practice in minutes, whenever you can find them—five or ten before school, after lunch, between chores. Spread the practice throughout the day, and music will become a part of your life."

Erskine practiced this throughout his life and even wrote *Helen of Troy*, his most famous work, as he rode on streetcars to and from his work at the university.[4]

I have personally found this method to be an indispensable aid. One of my goals is in the area of memorizing Scripture. I've managed to memorize many books of the New Testament on my fifteen-minute coffee breaks and during my lunch hour. Taking it in little snatches makes it not only enjoyable but also a change of pace that I look forward to.

3. *Learn to take breaks as you pursue your goals.* Edwin C. Bliss writes, "To work for long periods without taking a break is not an effective use of time. Energy decreases, boredom sets in, and physical stress and tension accumulate. Switching for a few minutes to something physical—isometric exercises, walking around the office, even changing from a sitting position to a standing position for a while—can provide relief.

"Merely resting, however, is often the best course, and you should not think of a 'rest' break as a poor use of time. Not only will being refreshed increase your efficiency, but relieving tension will benefit your health."[5]

4. *Remove the irritants.* Irritants can stymie goal-setting and goal-reaching. When a situation that repeats itself daily or weekly barges into your life situation, sometimes the best thing to do is remove it, or find a way around it.

In *Getting Organized* Stephanie Winston says, "Eliminating or ameliorating the many regular irritations, the small insults, that affect your life can provide important results. For example, an unpleasant daily route to work through an industrial wasteland may prove depressing. Waiting in line is anathema to many people. Take a few minutes to analyze the irritants that stud your day, and then revise your schedule or your environment in whatever ways possible to at least soften their effect."[6]

If a time waster for you is standing in lines, dissipate the boredom by using it for reaching other goals—praying, memorizing a verse of Scripture, even reading a book. If one of your goals is to read Charles Hodge's *Systematic Theology*, it might be difficult to motivate yourself when you have free time. But what about while on the bus, or during your coffee break, or in snatches in the bathroom? It can make that time profitable and even fulfilling!

5. *Use the word* no. It's short. It doesn't always feel good when it comes out. But later, after you've used it, you'll find it carries a terrific afterglow.

And it will help you keep moving single-mindedly toward the end of the furrow.

A tip on time: Spend some time in prayer and meditation, and ask yourself, *What do I want to do with my life? What do I want to accomplish?* Write down at least one thing for every major activity and every relationship you're involved in.

NOTES

1. Roger Ricklefs and Udayan Gupta, "Traumas of the New Entrepreneur," *Wall Street Journal,* May 10, 1989, p. B1.

2. Mark Porter, *The Time of Your Life* (Wheaton, Ill.: Victor, 1983), p. 155.

3. Gordon MacDonald, *Ordering Your Private World* (Nashville: Thomas Nelson, 1984), p. 91.

4. Quoted in *Bits and Pieces,* March 1982.

5. Edwin C. Bliss, *Getting Things Done* (New York: Scribner, 1976).

6. Stephanie Winston, *Getting Organized* (New York: Warner, 1978), p. 50.

18

Productivity or People?

*I have two [priorities]: God and my neighbor. They
are not in sequence. It is not love God for a certain
amount of time and to a certain degree and then love
my neighbor. It is love God and love my neighbor. Do
them both. Christ is saying, "Put God first." He is
also saying, "Put your neighbor first."*
—J. Grant Howard, *Balancing Life's Demands*

An incident from my college days magnified in my
mind what is really important. I and several friends
went off skiing in winter in the Poconos of Pennsylvania.
On the way out it began to snow. Soon a pure white veil
lay on the roads.

I drove my 1965 cream-colored Mustang hurriedly,
a little nervous, but impatient to get to the ski area. We
came around a curve, and up ahead of us a blue Falcon
was making a left turn. Over a hundred yards separated
us, so I didn't slow down. We were going about forty-
five miles an hour, probably too fast for the snowy
conditions.

I kept barreling along, murmuring that the idiot in
the Falcon should turn. At fifty yards he still hadn't
made his move. My brother said, "You better slow
down, Mark."

I answered, "No problem. No one's coming. He'll
turn."

185

He didn't turn. In the end, I slammed on the brakes, smashed into his rear end, and ended up with a $300 fender-bender. The Falcon lost a rear tail light.

When I got to a service station I called Dad and told him the news. He asked immediately, "Is everyone all right?"

All I could think of was the car. "It's really bad, Dad. The fender's all crumpled up, and the left light's punched out, and . . ."

Dad interrupted me. "Mark, is everyone OK?"

I stammered on. "The service station guy says it's a good three-hundred, four-hundred, Dad. Where will I get that kind of money?"

Dad broke in again. "IS EVERYONE ALL RIGHT?"

I stopped and thought. *Of course everyone was OK.* I told him.

He answered "Then don't worry about the car. Cars can be fixed. Sometimes people can't."

I was thirty years old before I understood what he really said to me.

How much do people matter to you? How much does being productive mean to you? And which is more important:

1. Knowing the state of the economy; reading the sports page; solving your son's arithmetic problem with him.

2. Giving 10 percent of your income at church; negotiating with your daughter a new allowance; paying the bills on time.

3. Watching your favorite show; watching your wife's favorite show; getting to bed early just to talk.

4. Reading a spiritual life book; applying the principles of the spiritual life book to your life; discussing your spiritual life with your wife and praying about it.

5. Cutting the lawn in an hour; letting your six-year-old son try for an hour, then doing it yourself in the next hour; cutting the lawn in two hours with your six-year-old-son helping you push.

6. Sorting the wash; sorting the wash with your eight-year-old granddaughter helping; burning the wash and buying new clothes (with your granddaughter).

OK, we did get a little weird there toward the end. But think about it. Which is more important—productivity (getting the job done in the most efficient way, using the least time with the greatest results) or people (doing the job with a child or friend and getting it done, or half done, or undone, or having to start over three times because they messed it up the first two)?

Not an Easy Answer

It's not easy to find an answer. Since the Industrial Revolution of the nineteenth century, man has learned that cost-efficient production makes money. Fast. And with money you can do a lot of good for yourself and others.

But in the process, we've also discovered that the fierce competition of the marketplace can leave people not only behind but smashed flat in the dust. We "step on one another," "knife one another in the back," "put one another down," and "rub each other's nose in it." It's not always a pretty picture.

Jesus made God's priorities in the area of people very clear. If you look at His statement in Matthew 22:37-39 about the "greatest commandment," you might come away thinking God is first, people are second. But J. Grant Howard offers a different conclusion on the basis of Jesus' words "the second is like it."

"What does this passage teach us about priorities? I have two: God and my neighbor. They are not in sequence. It is not love God for a certain amount of time and to a certain degree and then love my neighbor. It is love God and love my neighbor. Do them both. Christ is saying, 'Put God first.' He is also saying, 'Put your neighbor first.' Christ is saying, 'Give God top priority.' He is also saying, 'Give your neighbor top priority.'

"It is my responsibility to love God and at the same time my responsibility to love my neighbors."[1]

Isn't it interesting that productivity doesn't even enter into Christ's thought here at all? It's not, "Love the Lord your God with all your heart, soul, mind, and might by getting a lot done for Him, and love your neighbor as yourself, producing as much as you can in the shortest time possible."

Yet, to look at today's hurry-scurry society, you'd think productivity was paramount.

We work fifty, sixty, seventy hours a week.

After that we hurry off to the spa, club, or court to get our bodies in shape. Then . . .

the kids have to be at swim team, in ballet, playing in the chess tournament, doing the Sunday school play, keeping up with MYF, and getting good grades. Then . . .

on Saturday we must cut the lawn, weed the garden, clean up the kitchen, plant the roses, play a round of tennis, hit the pool, read the summer sizzler, cook out, grab a video, no, make that two, read the paper before bed, and, oh, yeah, read a few verses before Sunday when . . .

we speed off to Sunday school, arrive ten minutes late, vow to be on time next week, hurry through the Sunday school lesson, sit through the church service, sing in the choir, take notes in the bulletin, mark up our Bibles, cram the notes into the flyleaf, think up something nice to say to the pastor on the way out, read the committee minutes in our church mailbox, speed read the other mail, listen to Deacon Bill tell us about the new evangelistic program that we should be involved in, make a decision about whether Sally can go to the teen luncheon, hurry to get out of our choir robes, find the car, wait to get out of the parking lot, speed home, read the Sunday paper, cram through the booklet for tonight's discipleship fellowship, make dinner, eat dinner, have a family quiet time . . .

Hey, I'm getting tired! And tomorrow we start in on ten hours at the office and—

Good grief, has anyone fed the cat?

Where do the people fit into our schedules? "Oh," you say, "they're there. All over the place."

Uh-huh. And what was said? What was done? Do you remember? Do you care to remember? Do you remember to care to remember?

OK, I'M GETTING OBNOXIOUS, BUT . . .

I'll admit that. I can be murder sometimes. Let me just offer a few thoughts on what Christians are finding out about people.

It takes time to build friendships.

Jeri Sweany told me, "As I have gotten older and hopefully a bit wiser I am realizing that you never have enough time to do all that you want to do. The important thing is to do the best you can with the time God has given you. Just in the past year I am realizing how important relationships are and that it takes time to establish good relationships."

It takes time to understand where people are and what they're thinking.

These words in *Fortune* magazine's article "How CEOs Manage Their Time" are instructive: A good executive "might wander down the hall on his way to a meeting and never make it to the meeting. He gets diverted over here for two minutes, and then talks with someone else for five minutes, and then races across the hall to catch somebody else for another minute, and finally arrives at the scheduled meeting twenty minutes late. The time-management folks would gasp. But what's happening is this: As the stimuli pour at him all day long, his clear sense of where the company is trying to go enables him to be highly efficient in choosing what to react to and what to ignore."[2]

It takes time to minister effectively to people. Jesus spent three years discipling twelve men full time. That was every day—living, eating, sleeping, and walking together. Today, we make up charts that show how we can convert 4 billion people in twenty years by discipling someone new every six months, meeting about once a week one-on-one for an hour or two. Whom are we kidding?

Eileen Merrell told me what special activities are important to her. She listed three:

"1. Teens. One on one, group times, Sunday school. Many of my teens are now in their early 20s. Yet a few of them are still in my life, calls, visits, prayers. Why am I committed to them? I remember my teen years. I didn't know Jesus. I made some *stupid* mistakes that only Jesus could remove the pain from. I want to be here for teens, to introduce Jesus to them.

"2. Volunteering for odd jobs for school and church. Why? Because sometimes people look so burdened, and God's given me my health to serve Him.

"3. Friends—I want them to know Jesus. The price? Sometimes my rug doesn't get vacuumed, or we eat microwaved food instead of home cooked. It bothers me sometimes."

But it needn't. She's laying up treasure in heaven—investing her life in something that goes to heaven: people!

How Can You Give People Time?

How, then, can you get off the productivity treadmill and start loving people? Several thoughts.

1. *Learn to include your family and others in what you're doing.* Michael Green of Dallas Theological Seminary says, "I try to take my family with me whenever I

go out to preach. If I have to rake the leaves, I let my six-year-old daughter help. It takes twice as long, but we have fun raking leaves. My goal is not only productivity (to rake up leaves), but also people (to build a relationship with my daughter).

"One day when we were cutting the lawn, a bolt fell off the engine and I had to fix it. My daughter and I prayed about it. Then we fixed it. She saw prayer in action.

"If my wife is making cookies, she lets our daughter help. Again, it takes twice as long. But my wife's goal isn't just to make cookies, it's to build a relationship."

He offered a potent principle on time we all should heed: "The goal of time management is not productivity, but building relationships that build the kingdom of God."

2. *Strive to limit other activities.* Dr. Frank Minirth, well known psychiatrist and author, explained to me, "The most important principle is just to limit the number of things that you do. I devote the majority of my time to my family, then to my ministry, which is also my work. Almost everything I do involves my family."

He added, "People's lives are literally at stake. So many people come to us whose parents had no time to develop a nurturing relationship with them, and their lives have been seriously wounded. It is important that we minister first to our own families."

And one for the church:

3. *Encourage your church to make a conscious effort to limit the amount of meetings it holds.* Brent Brooks told me, "Everything in our culture pulls the family and people apart. The church puts everyone into different groups. In the church I'm involved in, we've worked to limit the number of meetings so that people can really minister. Let people make the choices who are closest to what's happening instead of having a committee do it.

Trust your leaders. Let them lead. Push the meetings out into the community, so people don't have to meet at the church all the time, but in their homes.

"We have three women's Bible studies designed to do evangelism because these women have the time. They're not involved in heavy church activities. They have time to focus on reaching their neighbors.

"People are excited and glad to be able to do the ministry themselves. One man some twenty years ago became a single parent. Now he has a significant ministry with single parents because he was trained and has the time and desire to serve.

"It comes down to this. Our format has allowed people time to spend with their families on Sunday nights, reaching their neighbors and building friendships, and have a real ministry to one another."

Jim Dethmer added, "In the typical church today you have so many services there's no chance to build real relationships. We decided to work on the basis of one main service per week, then meet in small groups at the convenience of the group."

How has it worked?

"People have responded most positively. Many have expressed appreciation to me about our emphasis on building relationships rather than meetings. People are reaching out to their neighbors. They now have the time.

"One example of the priority of relationships is something my wife and I did over Thanksgiving. We had a couple stay over the whole weekend. They live nearby. But we wanted to build a deeper friendship. So they stayed at our house and we had a whole week end together. That builds real intimacy."

This doesn't mean pastors should go to a wholesale restructuring of the church meetings and services. But they must evaluate: Are our present services doing the work of real discipleship? Are people ministering in the community and to one another? Or are people frustrated, burned out, moving on?

Whatever choices people make, they will remain with them for eternity.

A tip on time: Ask your wife, your husband, your children, your best friends how they feel about your "hurried" life-style. What steps might you take now to eliminate the rush and begin to be still long enough to hear the voice from the heart?

Notes

1. J. Grant Howard, *Balancing Life's Demands* (Portland, Oreg.: Multnomah, 1983), p. 44.

2. Ford S. Worthy, "How CEOs Manage Their Time," *Fortune*, January 18, 1988, p. 88.

19

Temporal Ease or True Rest?

Remember a long life of steady, consistent, holy labour will produce twice as much fruit as one shortened and destroyed by spasmodic and extravagant exertions; be careful and sparing of your strength when and where exertion is unnecessary.

—Catherine Mumford Booth,
letter to her husband,
General William Booth

Some of the kindest words start with **R**.

rest	reflect	rekindle (old dreams)
relax	renew	refurbish (the front room)
rehabilitate	revitalize	replay (the song)
refresh	rejuvenate	reminisce (over old times)
R and R	remember	

But ultimately that little word *rest* is the best. Like the ancient black woman said, explaining her easy chair posture, "When I works, I works hard. And when I rests, I rests loose."

James M. Barrie put it this way: "You must have been warned against letting the golden hours slip by; but some of them are golden only because we let them slip by."

REAL REST

But what is biblical rest?

The concept of "rest" runs throughout the Bible. God "rested" on the seventh day (Genesis 2:2). He gave us a "day of rest," the sabbath or seventh day. He speaks of a "spiritual rest" available to those who will obey (see Hebrews 3:11).

Tim Kimmel has done a fine study of spiritual rest in *Little House on the Freeway*. In his view, biblical rest has three basic components related to our personal needs. Let me put it into a little chart:

Need:	*Question:*	*Answer:*
Love	Am I loved?	Acceptance
Purpose	Do I matter?	Affirmation
Hope	Am I going anywhere?	Assurance

Kimmel suggests that God answers our tremendous need for love by offering us eternal and total acceptance in Christ. "Therefore, there is now no condemnation for those who are in Christ Jesus" (Romans 8:1).

He answers our need for purpose through affirmation. "'For I know the plans I have for you,' declares the Lord, 'plans to prosper you and not to harm you, plans to give you hope and a future'" (Jeremiah 29:11).

And He answers our need for hope by assuring us He's taking us to a perfect and heavenly destination. "He who began a good work in you will carry it on to completion until the day of Christ Jesus" (Philippians 1:6).

HOW DO YOU FIND REST?

How, then, do you find this rest in the midst of our out of control culture? Kimmel offers six stout pieces of advice:[1]

He says that first, *"we must maintain an attitude of forgiveness."* Bitterness and resentment sap the spirit. Only true forgiveness will ease the acidic fire in our souls. "Get rid of all bitterness, rage and anger, brawling and slander, along with every form of malice. Be kind and compassionate to one another, forgiving each other, just as in Christ God forgave you" (Ephesians 4:31-32).

Second, *"we must live our lives within the boundaries of God's word."* God's word is not just our guide through life; it's an indispensable operation manual for healthy living. Second Timothy 3:16-17 sums it well: "All Scripture is God-breathed and is useful for teaching, rebuking, correcting and training in righteousness, so that the man of God may be thoroughly equipped for every good work."

Third, *"everyday life must always be lived against the backdrop of eternity."* Keep before yourself the truth of Ecclesiastes: "Here is the conclusion of the matter: Fear God and keep his commandments, for this is the whole duty of man. For God will bring every deed into judgment, including every hidden thing, whether it is good or evil." Also, Romans 8:18: "I consider that our present sufferings are not worth comparing with the glory that will be revealed in us."

Fourth, we must recognize that *"accepting and serving are the best antidotes for suffering."* James's words in James 1:2-4 are memorable: "Consider it pure joy, my brothers, whenever you face trials of many kinds, because you know that the testing of your faith develops perseverance. Perseverance must finish its work so that you may be mature and complete, not lacking anything."

Fifth, *"we must discipline our desires."* Contentment comes through discipline. Limiting yourself to what is necessary is crucial to survival. "But godliness with contentment is great gain. For we brought nothing into the world, and we can take nothing out of it. But if we have food and clothing, we will be content with that" (1 Timothy 6:6-8).

Sixth, *"we must manage our resources."* Kimmel speaks of our calling, our convictions, and our capabilities as three important resources we must manage for the kingdom of God. Paul pictures it this way in 1 Corinthians 4:1-2: "So then, men ought to regard us as servants of Christ and as those entrusted with the secret things of God. Now it is required that those who have been given a trust must prove faithful."

To some degree we have discussed all of these truths in this book. Applying them in the pull and push of daily living will go far to bring true spiritual rest to our lives.

MORE APPLICATIONS

But let me offer you several other specific applications beyond this that also relate to the rest we can gain for our souls.

1. *Remember the 80/20 rule.* In my research, I repeatedly came across Velfredo Pareto's rule. He was a nineteenth-century Italian economist and sociologist who discovered that 20 percent of the people in Italy possessed 80 percent of the wealth. This led to further discoveries of an 80/20 rule, which Mark Porter helps to amplify:

"80 percent of the sales volume is generated from 20 percent of the product line.

"80 percent of the sales come from 20 percent of the customers.

"80 percent of the total sick leave is concentrated in 20 percent of the employees.

"80 percent of a pastor's time is spent with 20 percent of the people.

"80 percent of the giving comes from 20 percent of the members.

"80 percent of the relevant information can be transmitted with 20 percent of the words."[2] (Oooo, that one hurts!)

What does this have to do with rest? Just this: many Christian leaders and laymen spend hours in frustration, aggravation, and even resentment about . . .

> all those in the church (or family, workplace, and so on) who barely serve (or don't at all),
>
> all those in the church who barely give (or don't at all),
>
> all those who never quite get their life together spiritually (and then continually bother you about it),
>
> all those who drain resources without giving back.

It can be a stifling, enervating feeling. The way out is to begin to understand human nature and the reality in which we live. Even Jesus preached something akin to the 80/20 rule in the parable of the soils (maybe it was 75/25 for Him). Remember the four soils on which seed was sown? Only one bore fruit. The rest either didn't get it, gave up, or flaked off!

The point is, stop berating yourself and the 20 percent who do give, serve, love, and grow because of the 80 percent who don't! Let it be, and get on with the business of real discipleship with the 20 percent who want to go all the way with Jesus.

2. *Learn to trust others and delegate.* It's not God's will that you do everything, most of the things, or even many things. For Mary and Martha, Jesus said only one thing was necessary. Mary had "chosen the good part" (see Luke 10:38-42), and it wouldn't be taken away from her.

One executive manager, who also happens to be my father, told me, "Early on I learned to delegate things to people and trust them to get the job done." That may be part of the reason for his own success as one of the first American presidents of a subsidiary of Mitsubishi Heavy Industries, the giant Japanese corporation. As a witness to it, I'm always amazed at how composed he remains in the midst of problems, how much time he spends with church, family, and friends, and how much work he still gets done.

3. *Know yourself.* Gordon MacDonald recommends understanding your own rhythms, your own limits, and your own needs and desires so that you can apply them in your use and scheduling of time. It makes no sense to schedule the hardest, most mentally demanding tasks during your 3:00-4:00 P.M. down period. Or to have your quiet time at an hour when you're normally groggy, grumpy, and grubby.

A fascinating article in *Time* revealed research done by Pioneer Frontier Explorations on the stresses of long term isolation.[3] Stephania Follini went underground in Carlsbad, New Mexico, for 131 days and lived in a 20-foot by 12-foot Plexiglas module. There was no contact with the sun, clocks, or anything close to normal time keeping.

The result? Follini's "internal clocks" went berserk, with workdays ranging from twenty-eight to forty-eight hours, and sleeping periods lasting up to twenty-four hours.

However, the research has proved helpful, especially to investigators who studied the destruction of the Challenger shuttle and the Three Mile Island and Chernobyl nuclear reactor disasters. They "found that in each case, critical errors were made by people struggling with unusual work schedules and lack of sleep. The two nuclear accidents happened in the wee hours of the morning. Similarly, most truck wrecks related to fatigue occur between 2:00 A.M. and 4:00 A.M."

All this has led some employers to consider giving their employees more flexible schedules in line with their "internal clocks."

Knowing and understanding your own limitations and rhythms will go a long way to enabling us to experience true spiritual rest. When you understand your own weaknesses and strengths, you can use your time more effectively because you cease doing the things you're not equipped to do, and you get on with the important matters God designed you for.

General William Booth, founder of the Salvation Army, once received a letter from his wife that is most telling. She said,

"Your Tuesday's notes arrived safe, and I was rejoiced to hear of the continued prosperity of the work, though sorry you were so worn out; I fear the effect of all this excitement and exertion upon your health, and though I would not hinder your usefulness, I would caution you against an injudicious prodigality of your strength.

"Remember a long life of steady, consistent, holy labour will produce twice as much fruit as one shortened and destroyed by spasmodic and extravagant exertions; be careful and sparing of your strength when and where exertion is unnecessary."[4]

4. *Consider taking naps.* In an article in *Parade* magazine, Morton Hunt writes, "Dr. [David] Dinges and scientists at sleep-research centers have found that napping is not only healthful and beneficial but also, for many people, can make the difference between vigor and lethargy—even life and death."[5]

So who ought to take naps? Hunt says, "Most of us. Brain-wave tests and other studies show that human beings have an inherent tendency to sleep twice a day—an urgent need to sleep for many hours at nighttime and a less-urgent need to sleep briefly in midafternoon."[6]

We shouldn't overdo it. But even as a child, I remember going to work with my grandfather when I visited him on vacations. He was a construction superintendent with heavy job site responsibilities. We drove around in his truck from site to site checking things out.

At the time I couldn't understand why, but each afternoon he'd pull the truck over in some shady area and take a forty-five minute nap. Now I'm sure it was that "refreshing sleep" that gave him the energy to keep on top of hundreds of workers and several projects all at once.

So when is it best to take a nap? Hunt quotes psychiatrist Martin Orne of the University of Pennsylvania: "A nap taken *before* you're very tired will prevent fatigue." Anywhere from fifteen minutes to an hour can be effective.

Still, even learning to be quiet is helpful. In his home, Tim Kimmel declares "Quiet Night" once a month or so. No stereos on. No TV. "Nothing that makes noise," he says, "is allowed to come on." He wants his children to learn to find solace and comfort in the calm and quiet of an evening—"to listen to the sound effects of heaven."

5. *The power of music.* Berthold Auerbach said, "Music washes away from the soul the dust of everyday life." Hans Christian Andersen thought of it this way: "Where words fail, music speaks." And Martin Luther, a great lover of music, who set the words of "A Mighty Fortress Is Our God" to the tune of a popular drinking song of his day, said, "Music is the art of the prophets, the only art that can calm the agitations of the soul; it is one of the most magnificent and delightful presents God has given us."

How many times I have come home, stretched out on the couch, and listened to some favorite band or composer. There's refreshment, joy, and power in music. King David knew it well. The whole book of Psalms was, at one time, the songbook of Israel.

6. *Buy up snippets of time.* Roy Zuck of Dallas Theological Seminary told me, "I encourage students to use small bits of time to read, think, and so on. It's amazing how much a person can read while getting

dressed in the morning, while waiting for long traffic lights to change."

I have found that I look forward to such things as . . .

> standing in lines,
>
> sitting in doctors' offices,
>
> sitting on hold on the phone,
>
> waiting for my wife to get dressed,
>
> driving in the car.

It's all prime time to think through some project, memorize a Scripture verse, review a verse, read something from a book I'm carrying (in expectation of just such a situation), and, above all, to pray. There are a multitude of things to pray about during those "still, waiting moments." What? Pray for . . .

> specific needs you're aware of,
>
> the people around you, their salvation, spiritual lives,
>
> your church, family, friends, self,
>
> world conditions,
>
> missionaries,
>
> religious schools and training centers,
>
> authors, speakers, pastors, co-workers, celebrities (why not pray for the people you see in the headlines at the grocery checkout counter?).

What could Paul have meant by praying without ceasing, if not the act of "buying up snippets of time" to pray for the work of the kingdom? It's easy to let those snippets become clogged with worry. So stop, trust, and begin using those snippets for glory.

7. *Double up on time.* There are many activities we do that require only partial concentration. A mother can help a child with homework while sewing a button onto a shirt. She can pray with a friend while cooking

dinner, crochet while watching television, exercise while listening to the radio. A father can listen to a preaching tape while driving to work, learn a new language (on tape) while shaving, pray while taking a shower. It takes organization to do these things, but God is a God of order, not confusion (1 Corinthians 14:33).

8. *Eliminate the activities you have to force.* This is true of many of our activities—sometimes even true of church meetings. Dave Kruegar asks the question, "If we have to keep pumping it up, is it worth it?" If the pastor has to plead, cajole, and wheedle to get people to come to the latest seminar, training meeting, and whatnot, why do it in the first place? Why not concentrate on those things that people both need and want?

9. *Recognize your habits.* Many people spend time worrying about the things they don't do or haven't done because they try to do them at the wrong times, or in the wrong way. There's no set biblical pattern for such things as church services, having a quiet time, how you serve in the church, when to study the Bible, or how often you pray. There are guidelines in some cases, but, more often than not, God supplies the principle and the Spirit helps us tailor it to our lives.

Gordon MacDonald writes, "A careful study of my work habits has revealed an important insight. There are various tasks I accomplish best at certain times and under certain conditions.

"For example, I do not work effectively for my Sunday preaching during the early days of the week. Two hours of study on Monday are relatively worthless, while one hour on Thursday or Friday is almost priceless. I simply concentrate better."[7]

Not Beyond Any of Us

The rich fool said, "Take your ease; eat, drink, and be merry." Some of us want ease. But what we need is rest, God's rest. It's far better than materialism, worldly pleasures, and hurry. It's the thing that helps you swim steady when life flicks a briny wave into your face and, before you've had a chance to spit it out, promises to keep flickering until you've drowned or are ready to jump out.

A tip on time: Take some time today to "rest." Put on some music. Listen to the words. Drift. Think. Meditate. Pray. Nap. See if taking the time doesn't refresh.

NOTES

1. See Tim Kimmel, *Little House on the Freeway* (Portland, Oreg.: Multnomah, 1987), pp. 52, 56, 71, 82, 107, 117, 134.

2. Mark Porter, *The Time of Your Life* (Wheaton, Ill.: Victor, 1983), p. 135.

3. *Time*, June 5, 1989, pp. 66-68.

4. Harold Begbie, *Life of General William Booth* (New York: MacMillan, 1920), p. 178.

5. Morton Hunt, "What a Difference a Nap Makes," *Parade* (January 29, 1989), p. 16.

6. Ibid.

7. Gordon MacDonald, *Ordering Your Private World* (Nashville, Tenn.: Thomas Nelson, 1984), p. 87.

20

Frustration or Freedom?

Therefore, since we are surrounded by such a great cloud of witnesses, let us throw off everything that hinders and the sin that so easily entangles, and let us run with perseverance the race marked out for us.
—Hebrews 12:1

I asked a writer's group if any of them had any suggestions about taming the time crunch. Marilyn Marx, a homemaker with grown children in Annapolis, Maryland, told me, "I'm not celebrating Christmas this year. My grown kids and husband and self are going to the beach for three days. No gifts, no decorations, no cookies. This year's view of Christmas (by me) is closer to what the holiday was meant to be—a time of peace and meditation."

I don't know how my six-year-old would react to that one, but for some families it might be an idea whose time has come. My own family has decided to pick names out of a hat this year and buy presents only for the one whose name they picked. It will cut down on spending—which usually does our budget in each year—and time spent on the mall treadmill.

Marilyn also suggested some other hints: (1) use postcards instead of letters—you don't have to fill in as much, and people like them; (2) don't even read junk mail—throw it away, or, if you have a woodburning heater, use it to start the fire; (3) say no to requests you can't handle, and don't explain why—it avoids wheedling.

THE GOAL

What is the goal of all these time-saving devices? Freedom.

From what? Guilt. Overinvolvement. Shoddy workmanship. Poor performance. Arguments. Anger. Resentment.

And why? To be set free so you can serve God with excellence. Help others with exhilaration. Give with cheerfulness. Enjoy the good things in life. Carve out a moment for yourself . . . to think . . . to appreciate . . . to admire . . . to stare out the window and drift.

Time enough! That's what we really need. How to get it? Choose freedom a la Bible. The Bible offers the way out of frustration into freedom. How? Through the truth.

"If you hold to my teaching, you are really my disciples. Then you will know the truth, and the truth will set you free" (John 8:31-32).

ABIDING

The way to freedom is through knowing the truth. The way to know the truth is through abiding in Christ's word. We've all heard it many times. But what does it mean?

To "abide" means "to remain" or "to continue in" something.[1] Jesus meant, "If you steadfastly continue applying my Word to your life, you shall know the truth."

Isn't that interesting—"abiding" leads to knowing the truth. You might think it was the other way around. Knowing the truth leads to abiding. But knowing God's truth has a strange twist to it. God does not reveal His truth in strictly intellectual, mental terms. His truth involves the whole person—mind, emotions, will, soul, spirit. Biblical truth is not just factual, or in the form of law, maxim, or principle. In a sense, you can't understand biblical truth until you've experienced it in daylight. It's like marriage: you don't really know what it's like till you've been there. Or the excitement of winning a Superbowl: who could explain it better than someone who's been on the Superbowl gridiron?

Biblical truth is rooted in experience. That's why the writer to the Hebrews said, "Anyone who lives on milk, being still an infant, is not acquainted with the teaching about righteousness. But solid food is for the mature, who by constant use have trained themselves to distinguish good from evil" (Hebrews 5:13-14). "By constant use" we train ourselves "to discern good and evil." You must use it to understand it.

WHY DOES THE TRUTH SET US FREE?

But what is it about truth that sets people free?

Ever been immobilized by an irrational fear? Ever been knocked down by a vicious rumor or lie? Ever feel guilty about something you know you shouldn't feel guilty about—like buying yourself a beautiful dress, or going out to an expensive restaurant, or failing to witness to everyone you cross paths with, or reading your Bible for only fifteen minutes on Monday instead of thirty? Ever think you've lost your salvation, or that God hates you, or that God is totally fed up with you even though you're trying very hard to walk closely to Him?

All those situations can be solved by knowing and applying the truth. A. W. Tozer wrote, "Much Christianity since the days of Christ has been grim and severe. And the cause has been the same—an unworthy or inadequate view of God. . . .

"From a failure properly to understand God comes a world of unhappiness among good Christians even today. The Christian life is thought to be a glum, unrelieved cross-carrying under the eye of stern Father who expects much and excuses nothing. He is austere, peevish, highly temperamental and extremely hard to please. The kind of life which springs out of such libelous notions must of necessity be but a parody on the true life in Christ. . . .

"The truth is that God is the most winsome of all beings and His service one of unspeakable pleasure. He is all love, and those who trust Him need never know anything but that love. He is just, indeed, and He will not condone sin; but through the blood of the everlasting covenant He is able to act toward us exactly as if we had never sinned. Toward the trusting sons of men His mercy will always triumph over justice."[2]

How to Become Free in the Area of Time

How, then, do you become more free to gain back the time you wish you had but don't? Many of the principles we've already talked about directly impact our freedom in Christ. But let me amplify and suggest several more thoughts.

1. *Deal with encumbrances.* Hebrews 12:1-2 speaks to the need to strip down in order to run a good race. "Therefore, since we are surrounded by such a great cloud of witnesses, let us throw off everything that hinders and the sin that so easily entangles, and let us run with perseverance the race marked out for us. Let us fix our eyes on Jesus, the author and perfecter of our faith, who for the joy set before him endured the cross, scorning its shame, and sat down at the right hand of the throne of God."

The word for "everything that hinders" means "weight, burden, encumbrance"[3]—anything that slows you down in running your race for Christ. Since the next phrase uses the word "sin," I take encumbrance to mean anything that is neutral in a moral sense but does not advance the cause of the kingdom and your walk with Christ. It can be anything—music that occupies your mind and drains off high and holy thoughts; sports; hobbies; too much time with books, three-dollar novels, and junk reading; snacking; too much time on the phone; and above all, television. One of the best ways to get more time to do everything you want to do is this: punch the television switch, and leave it off.

Doug White delivers packages for UPS five days a week. He leaves home at 8:10 A.M. and gets back around 8:10 P.M. "Not many hours left after that," he says.

"But you can make some sacrifices. I used to sit down and watch a whole football game—four hours straight. Sunday and Monday evenings. No more. Now I just watch a show in the late evening with the high- lights. That's all you want to see anyway sometimes. My wife encourages me to watch. She knows I need that release."

I asked him what else he did in the evenings. "One thing I used to do was read the paper—cover to cover. I almost got on autopilot. Just read everything. But I stopped. I have to put it down and spend an hour just talking with my wife. We don't even watch television. Cuddle. Joke around. That kind of stuff. It's important."

That's freedom.

2. *Deal with sin.* I'm not trying to put anyone on a guilt trip, but a large part of the modern day time crunch for Christians is plain old everyday variety sin. Gossiping on the phone can kill off an hour before you know it. The greed to buy more costs both in time and money. God is not a God of disorder, but many house- holds look like the devil's playground in that respect. You can't find anything because it's total confusion.

What sin should you start with? The "Seven Deadly Ones" are a good place. What are they? Pride, covetous- ness, lust, anger, gluttony, envy, and sloth. Spot some- one in a time crunch, and chances are you'll find one of those seven peeking out from under his rapid-moving psyche. Not in all cases, but taking a hard look at your life—on a daily basis—can help considerably.

3. *Learn some basic time-saving techniques.* What are they? Try these on for size.

The "To Do" List. We've all heard about how Charles Schwab, the millionaire industrialist, paid Ivy Lee, a management consultant, $25,000 when the latter showed him the beauty of the "To Do" List. But famous as the illustration is, for many of us, the principle hasn't taken hold. Many people don't use it. Yet, it's a very helpful timesaving tool. How, then, does it work?

At the beginning of each day (or better yet, the night before), write down all the things you want to do that day. After you've made your list, give each one a priority rating: A = important; B = not so important; C = unimportant. Then go back to your A's and list them in order of priority. Leave your B's till later. And you may never want to do your C's, so don't worry about them.

Finally, now that your A's are order, start doing them in order of importance.

That's all there is to it. It was worth $25,000 to Charles Schwab in the early 1900s.

An appointment book. What a timesaver! And how simple. You no longer need to think back and remember. It's written down right on the date.

I have one that fits into my top left pocket. It's less than three inches high and two inches wide. It covers the whole year. But I write down more than appointments in it. It has blank pages for flitting ideas and thoughts. I can write them down and not forget them. There's another page for prayer requests. Another lists books I've read reviews of that I'd like to pick up at the library. Still another blank page lists—for me as a writer—ideas for books, poems, short stories. I don't have to try to "keep it in my mind." I can write it down the moment I think of it.

My little book also has a place for phone numbers. It provides maps, phone area codes, charts of time zones, travel distances, a temperature scale (Fahrenheit to Centigrade), conversion tables (American to metric), and other little doodads very useful in a time crunch.

Get one. Use it. You'll find it a third lobe for your brain.

Consolidate like items. Many items can be consolidated so that you do them all in one space of time. Pile up the bills and pay a group of them once or twice a month. Return all phone calls at a certain time of day rather than making them one at a time. While shopping, remember to make a list before you go. Gather up all the other errands, like taking the shoes to the cobbler and the shirts to the laundry, and then do it all in one big haul. Develop a file system that fits you and your needs. Keep like things in alphabetical order and in files under titles like insurance, tax returns, church, lease, refrigerator, and so on.

Use services. Changing Times featured an article that suggested, "Anything you can do, someone else can do faster—and that includes uncluttering your life. For $40 an hour, organizing consultant Sue McMillan will make order out of the chaos in your home office (three hours), child's room (three hours), or kitchen (six hours). Organizers are in such demand that the National Association of Professional Organizers, founded in 1985 with fewer than ten members, now has nearly 200."[4]

There were other suggestions in the same article:

> Make use of mobile laundry, car-cleaning, and tailor enterprises.
>
> Buy by catalog.
>
> Get all your prescriptions at one pharmacy.
>
> Combine bank accounts. (Instead, one each for hubby and wife, swallow that masculine pride and feminist ardor and go onesies.)

Deposit your paycheck automatically through your company.

Use your bank's "Automatic Bill Paying" system.

These services aren't for everyone. But for those who desire, they'll kill a crunch in a pinch.

Use labor-saving technology. Like "no show" carpets that don't require constant vacuuming and steam cleaning; stay-pressed shirts; new microwave ovens; low maintenance clothing; answering machines; VCR movies (better than watching "whatever's on"); and car telephones. Of the latter, Dr. Joe Werner says, "It's indispensable. I use it to conduct all types of business."

Of course, such things can go too far and you can end up in an even a greater time crunch if you're not careful. But wise, prayerful selection and buying can free up a lot of time for kingdom and personal pursuits.

4. *Move that paperwork.* A good rule of thumb is "Handle paper only once." Deal with it. Move it on. Stephanie Winston says, "There are only three things that can be done with a piece of paper: it can be thrown away; something can be done about it, such as writing a letter or making a phone call; or it can be temporarily put away."[5] But you must refuse to let it pile up, either on your desk at work, or in your home.

5. *Use your creativity.* In fact, ask God for help. In preparing this book, I was swamped with research material and was unsure of how to organize it. I prayed about it, and a day later I had a solution. I made photocopies of every quote I wanted to use, one copy for each example. I then laid out legal size sheets with the title of each chapter on the floor. After that, I went through the pile (about three inches thick) and divided up the supporting material by reading it briefly and laying it on the appropriate chapter title. I ended up with almost thirty little piles instead of one huge one. Writing the book became not only easier, but a joy.

Another example comes from O. W. Rollins, one-time Georgia farm boy who became president and chairman of the multimillion-dollar Rollins, Inc. When he was a boy, his grandmother "required everyone leaving the house to carry two empty pails with them, and, upon returning, bring two pails of water from the well."[6] Not only were they never without enough water, but no one ever had to make a special trip to the well—and thus, gobble up valuable time!

A tip on time: What areas of your life now are a frustration? What steps might you take to get more freedom? Take a half hour to discuss it tonight with your family. What encumbrances and sins might you eliminate?

NOTES

1. See *"meno,"* William F. Arndt and F. Wilbur Gingrich, *A Greek and English Lexicon of the New Testament* (Chicago: The U. of Chicago Press, 1957), pp. 504-5.

2. A. W. Tozer, "A God Who Is Easy to Please," *Discipleship Journal*, no. 47, 1988, p. 10.

3. See *"onkon,"* Arndt and Gingrich, p. 555.

4. Janet Bodnar, "33 Great Ways to Simplify Your Life," *Changing Times*, June 1989, p. 28.

5. Stephanie Winston, *Getting Organzied* (New York: Warner, 1978), p. 65.

6. Quoted in *Bits and Pieces*, February 1979.

21

Quantity or Quality?

Only fraud and deceit are ever in a hurry. Take time for all things; haste makes waste.

—Benjamin Franklin

Pete Reiser, an outfielder with the Brooklyn Dodgers in the 1940s, built a reputation on his hair-raising crashes into outfield walls snagging long drives. Frank Gifford writes in *Gifford on Courage* about one game in July 1942.

"Brooklyn was leading the league by 13½ games and the Cardinals were in town. It was the second game of a doubleheader, there was no score and it was in extra innings. Enos Slaughter belted a ball deep to center field. Racing for it, Reiser thought, 'If I don't get it, it's a triple and there could go the game.'

"He slammed into the wall at full speed, dropped the ball and knocked himself out. In the hospital, he learned he had a fractured skull. 'Was I being foolhardy in going after that ball the way I did?' Reiser asked years later. 'After all, we had a 13½ game lead. . . . You can slow up in those circumstances, can't you? No, you can't. You slow up a half step and it's the beginning of your last ball game. You can't turn it on and off any time you want to. Not if you take pride in yourself.'"[1]

A CONTRAST

In contrast to that praiseworthy commitment to quality performance, Dick Eastman laments, "Much of society has forgotten to persevere. We live in an age of quitters. Society constantly seeks new methods to solve 'drop-out' problems in schools. America's armed forces utilize hundreds of psychiatrists in hopes of curtailing desertions. Executives of corporations flee busy cities to hippie communes where 'drop-outs' congregate.... Few have a striving spirit like that of Raphael. Once he was questioned, 'What is your greatest painting?' He smiled, saying, 'My next one.'"[2]

Persistence. Perseverance. And above all, quality.

We speak of "quality control," "quality time," "quality products." Detroit knows the power of quality. When the Japanese car invasion came they thought they had nothing to worry about. But the Japanese had emphasized quality. Their long-lasting, low maintenance, easy-to-handle cars have made steady inroads into the American and world market.

For many of us it comes down to a choice: will I do what I do, pray what I pray, speak what I speak, and think what I think in a quantitative or a qualitative sense? A quantity of nonquality items equals trash. But a few quality products can not only make millions of dollars, they can benefit millions of people.

WHY IS QUALITY SO IMPORTANT IN OUR USE OF TIME?

Doing things qualitatively has important consequences in our mastery of time. One direct effect is that doing something right the first time means you don't have to do it a second time. Often when we do a shoddy job, we find we not only have to clean up the mess that resulted, but we have to start over again.

A second positive effect of quality work is that you feel a satisfaction you don't get when you know you haven't done your best. That means less time worrying, fretting, and feeling guilty—some of the major time-stealers.

A third effect is in the area of eternal value. What doesn't count for eternity, doesn't count. Period. When you learn to do quality work, it carries over into everything you do. You don't become a perfectionist; no, you become something far better: one who does all things to the glory of God. Quality means you have pleased God, and you will reap a reward for it not only in time but in eternity. That's the ultimate time-saver: what you have done will last!

What Is Quality?

What does it mean to do something in a quality way?

It's not perfectionism. That leads to frustration and obsessive correction of imperfections. No, qualitative performance is simply doing the best you can possibly do.

When Henry Kissinger was Secretary of State in the Nixon administration he repeatedly emphasized quality workmanship to his employees. Whenever an aide came to his desk with a report, Kissinger would gaze at him piercingly and ask, "Is this the best you can do?" The aide knew the answer and would leave, only to return the next day with a better version of the same report. Again, Kissinger would fiercely query, "Is this the very best you can do?" Out he'd go. Finally, the third day the aide would come in triumphant. "Yes, this is the very best I can do." "All right,' Kissinger would answer, "now I'll read it!"[3]

He demanded quality. And he got it.

Getting Quality into Your Life

What is the price of quality? Let me delineate six elements.

1. *Real quality calls for the power of the Spirit.* If you want to perform in the spiritual realm with quality, nothing less than the power of the Spirit will do. Look at Exodus 31:3a: "I have filled him with the Spirit of God, with skill, ability and knowledge in all kinds of crafts." God put within that workman a number of potent spiritual realities critical to quality control your life:

Wisdom: the ability to see the best way of doing the job

Understanding: the ability to put it all together

Knowledge: the background, research, and experience critical to success

Craftsmanship: the detail work so necessary to working with skill

Without the power of the Spirit we "can do nothing," as Jesus says, in John 15:5. We get that power through communion and reliance on God in faith.

2. *Real quality takes thought, prayer, and meditation.* I once read a prayer that said, "Lord, there's never enough time for everything. Help me to do a little less a little better." In the area of quality, less is more, and more is often less. By giving a project adequate thought, preparation, and meditation, qualitative results are not only possible but probable.

Before Arturo Toscanini became an orchestra conductor, he was a cellist. Because he was extremely nearsighted and didn't like bending close to the score sheets, he memorized not only his part, but the part of every other instrument as well. One night, the La Scala conductor fell ill. Someone suggested Toscanini take his place. The nineteen-year-old took the podium and promptly closed the score book, then conducted the entire program from memory. Tumultuous applause climaxed his performance.[4]

If that is the kind of thought and memory work that Toscanini put into musical productions, how much more the child of God for the kingdom of God!

3. *Real quality requires unhurried attention.* Two hundred years ago, Benjamin Franklin commented on the problem of hurry, saying, "Only fraud and deceit are ever in a hurry. Take time for all things; haste makes waste."

Many craftsmen of the eighteenth century produced quality products. Those who have visited Williamsburg, or collect antiques, know well the kind of workmanship that must have gone into such goods. Yet, how is it that such people without modern technology produced such magnificent work? Our ready answer is that they had more time.

But that's utterly untrue! They actually had much less. Their life spans were shorter. They didn't have modern machinery. Without good lighting their workday was curtailed.

Then how could they have made such remarkable contributions? It was all in the attitude: attention to detail, hard work, and a desire to produce the best possible commodity.

Larry Dyer, a pastor in Lake St. Louis, Missouri, put it this way: "I have to resist the temptation to sandwich in an appointment, or attempt more than is physically possible. Say I've got a 1:30 appointment for counseling and it's already 11:15 A.M. There are messages to answer, a stop at the bank, books to pick up at the Christian book store. With lunch to eat, I'll never make it! Far better to enjoy lunch, get ready, and be there relaxed at 1:30 than to come in 7 minutes late, worn, harried, and having lost my sanctification over the slowpoke!"

Larry concluded, "I have to remember I'm not the Omnipotent. I just work for Him."

4. *Real quality requires practice, effort, and energy.* Someone once asked Ignace Paderewski, the famed pianist, why he practiced six hours a day, every day, religiously. He answered, "If I miss one day's practice, I

notice it. If I miss two days, the critics notice it. If I miss three days, the audience notices it."[5]

William Barclay, the distinguished New Testament expositor, added to the same truth when he said, "I am no genius. I have a second-rate mind. Anything I have accomplished has been done by forcing myself to sit down and write for several hours every day."[6]

To produce anything that counts and lasts, that has an impact such as made by Paderewski and Barclay, will take practice, effort, energy. People will not remember how quickly you finished the job. But they will often recall how well it was done.

5. *Real quality takes heart.* A favorite Scripture is Colossians 3:23: "Whatever you do, work at it with all your heart." The Greek word used for heart is "soul,"[7] the involvement of every part of your being. It starts in the heart; spreads to the mind, emotions, and will; and comes out through the fingertips.

An Athenian sculptor named Phidias created the matchless figure of Athena to be placed in the Acropolis. One day he was working on the back of her head. As he chiseled, he was careful to draw out every strand of hair. Someone commented, "That figure is to stand a hundred feet high, with its back to the marble wall. Who will ever know what details you are putting behind there?" Phidias answered, "I will know."

The Christian could add, "And so would God."

6. *Real quality brings with it not only eternal but earthly rewards as well.* Nothing quite pleases a workman like a job well done, or a Sunday school teacher like a job well taught, or a wife like a kiss well rendered.

At the end of his life, Paul could write in good conscience and with genuine humility, "I have fought the good fight, I have finished the race, I have kept the faith. Now there is in store for me the crown of righteousness, which the Lord, the righteous Judge, will award to me on that day—and not only to me, but also to all who have longed for his appearing" (2 Timothy 4:7-8). He not only had the expectation of a good reward in heaven but the knowledge that he had done his best while in His Lord's service.

THE TIME CRUNCH AND QUALITY CONTROL

What, then, can be done to slow down and start doing things that last instead of things that lose? I see at least five applications.

1. *Ask God for direction about what work you should do.* Libbie Gutsche, a sixty-one year old wife and mother with three married daughters, has, over the years with her husband, been active in various ministries. At first they worked with international students, then spent fourteen years with college-career people. More recently they opened their home to unwed mothers with Bethany Christian Services. She told me, "In recent years the crush of time has not affected me because I learned early to pray long and hard over new opportunities as they arise. Things seem to be right if I wait long enough. God shows me what is important for me and what I should leave for others."

2. *Plan your day on paper.* Don't do it mentally. The lightest ink is better than the sharpest memory. This enables you to free your thoughts for the work at hand, rather than trying to remember the next step. You can use a "Day-Timer" or Higgins Productivity Software or a "To Do" list.

3. *Require quality from the people under you.* Especially in the church, there's a need to require people do one quality job rather than many shoddy jobs. It's better to have a few jobs done well than many done poorly.

One of my professors used to use an illustration about a cartoon with two frames. The first frame pictured Mrs. Brown applying for a teaching position in a local school. The principal told her, "Unfortunately, Mrs. Brown, we prefer teachers with a master's degree and you only have a B.A. Also, you have only one year of experience, and we prefer teachers with at least five. Finally, we expect you to study at least fifteen hours a week and you have indicated that with your family and so on you can only do ten. So we'll have to turn you down."

The next frame portrays the same teacher, only this time it's the principal as Sunday school superintendent trying to wangle her to take on the junior boys. He says, "I assure you, Mrs. Brown, degrees don't matter here. And as for your experience, that you have none makes no difference. You'll learn as you go along. Finally, many hours of study are not required. Less than a half hour a week should do. We're just looking for a willing heart."

The prof always concluded, "Do you know what the message of that cartoon is? 'In the church, anything is good enough for God!'"

How sad that we operate that way in the name of Christ.

I work with an editor at *Reader's Digest* who has sometimes sent a manuscript back to me five and six times before she felt we had it right. What I find is that I don't resent her penchant for perfection; rather, I revel in it. Through her guidance and help, I have learned to become a better, more exact writer. Her requiring quality of me has made me more aware of what it means to do things qualitatively all across the board.

4. *In the church, it's better to have a few or even one high-quality experience per week than many mediocre ones.* Gene Getz has built his ministry on church renewal and a concept of one centralized worship service per week with other meetings in homes at other times. "We don't want to put people in tension," he says. "So we schedule only one quality worship service per week."

This is not to say that pastors should go out and cut Sunday night and Wednesday night services, as well as others presently on the schedule. But some hard questions have to be asked:

Is the present service structure meeting needs?

Can we maintain quality amid quantity?

Do we have to make some choices to preserve integrity?

And above all,

Does the present schedule glorify God, or are we simply trying to keep a dead weight afloat?

5. *Use modern technology, especially the computer.* Five years ago I was afraid of computers. My experience in college with Fortran and punch cards made me wary. But after using IBM equipment in my work, I know well the power of the computer. Since getting a MacIntosh SE in my office at home my output has increased tenfold without sacrificing home and family time. Computers are not only fast, they're far more exact than any of us could ever be, and they're often easy to use. Apple Computers especially has made a science of "user-friendliness." I wouldn't trade my Mac for a whole stack of typewriters, address machines, file systems, or any other automated equipment.

THE BIG CHOICE

Ultimately, this choice of quality over quantity could be the most important one any of us ever make. Choosing quality will not only make our time productive but also enjoyable and memorable.

A tip on time: Take a hard look at what you're producing. Is it qualitative or not? If not, maybe you need to pull back and concentrate on doing one thing wholly rather than many things half-heartedly.

NOTES

1. Frank Gifford and Charles Mangel, *Gifford on Courage* (New York: Evans, 1988), pp. 24-25.
2. Dick Eastman, *No Easy Road* (Grand Rapids, Mich.: Baker, 1971), pp. 96-97.
3. Quoted in Dorothy Sarnoff, *Make the Most of Your Best* (Garden City, N.Y.: Doubleday, 1981).
4. James C. Humes, *Speaker's Treasury of Anecdotes About the Famous* (New York: Harper & Row, 1978), p. 137.
5. Humes, p. 68.
6. Quoted in *Christian Standard*, January 7, 1979.
7. See "*psyche*," William F. Arndt and F. Wilbur Gingrich, *A Greek and English Lexicon of the New Testament* (Chicago: U. of Chicago Press, 1957), pp. 901-2.

22

Jack of All Trades
or Master of One?

*Give me a man who says, "This one thing I do," like
Paul, and not, "These 50 things I dabble in."*
—D. L. Moody

Samuel Taylor Coleridge was a multitalented writer
and poet, with high intelligence and potent speaking
skills. Yet, William Barclay writes of this man's life:

"Coleridge is the supreme tragedy of undiscipline.
Never did so great a mind produce so little. He left Cambridge University to join the army; he left the army because he could not rub down a horse; he returned to
Oxford and left without a degree. He started a paper
called *The Watchman* which lived for ten numbers and
then died. It has been said of him: 'he lost himself in visions of work to be done, that always remained to be
done. Coleridge had every poetic gift but one—the gift of
sustained and concentrated effort.' In his head and in
his mind he had all kinds of books, as he said, himself,
'completed save for the transcription. I am on the even,'
he says, 'of sending to the press two octavo volumes.'
But the books were never composed outside of Coleridge's mind, because he would not face the discipline of
sitting down to write them out."[1]

CONCENTRATION OF EFFORT

It takes discipline to produce a qualitative, lasting result. But there's something more. I'd call it concentration of effort. Clearly, we can't do all we want to do; but we can concentrate on a few things, perhaps only one. It need not even be something stupendous, just that one thing that we give our lives to and which we end up giving a true quality treatment.

Few of us will ever have heard of Gerald Pereth of England. As a sailor in the British Merchant Navy he believed always in doing his best. He was put on KP duty peeling potatoes. Pereth decided if peeling potatoes was the job, then he would do it well. He carved those skins off like Michelangelo sculpting the Pieta. Soon, the cooks began boasting about the clean, eyeless potatoes he produced, until he had a reputation all over the navy.

What does Mr. Pereth do today? He's in business for himself—supplying select potatoes, peeled perfectly, to the classiest restaurants in London.[2]

That may not strike you as stupendous, but one of the big factors in the time crunch many Christians are experiencing is not only the problem of quantity and quality, but the simple problem of being spread too thin. There's a need to cut back and do one job right rather than two, three, four, or ten rotten.

I don't want to overlap what I've said in the previous chapter, but let me offer several important points.

1. *Become an expert at something.* I once heard a preacher say, "An expert is someone who knows no more than you do, but he has it better organized and uses slides."

True. But there is something to concentrating on one thing. George Washington Carver is quoted as asking God to tell him the secrets of the universe. God said that was too big; he should choose something smaller. So Carver asked to know the mysteries of the peanut.

Apparently God answered that one because Carver's discoveries are still with us today.

There is tremendous satisfaction in mastering a subject or developing your skills in one facet of life. Perhaps our time crunch is because we have opted for the forest rather than the tree, or the leaf, or even the stem. Instead of running around to a mass of activities, try concentrating on just one.

This applies especially to families with children. We parents desire the best for our kids, and rightly so. But we can all wear ourselves out by having too many places to run to, too much equipment to purchase, and too many performances to attend. Instead, pick out one or two and concentrate on doing them well.

2. *Learn to do one job in the church and do it well; then add if you want.* I heard this principle repeatedly from the people who filled out my questionnaire. Only take on more jobs in the church if you have one under control.

Paul said, "This one thing I do." The converse to that is, "These many things I don't do!"

Similarly, D. L. Moody wrote, "Give me a man who says, 'This one thing I do,' like Paul, and not, 'These 50 things I dabble in.'"

Resist the dabbling syndrome. You have to choose: will I have a quality ministry, or spread myself so thin that no one even feels its effect?

Judy Winter, a pastor's wife in Denver, Colorado, remarked to me, "In our last church, I decided not to sing in the choir. I had to prioritize, and I couldn't give it the work it deserved. I've learned that my first year in a church I only do one thing, usually join a circle. And no committees!"

Bill Tamulonis, to whom I've referred previously, said, "We limit the number of activities my wife and I are involved in to two per week. Right now we're involved in a class on marriage and our house church. We don't schedule anything else that meets regularly."

3. *Refuse to do something just because it's there.* The mountaineer climbed the mountain "because it was there." And many people take on jobs in the church "because if I don't do it, it won't get done." Maybe it's better to leave it undone!

Please understand, I'm not advocating a selfish outlook that says, "It doesn't coincide with my goals; therefore I'm not doing it." Rather, we need to have the same kind of servant attitude that Jesus had. Larry Dyer put it this way: "Time management insists that you force others to serve your considerations, but the Greatest Role Model said, 'The Son of Man did not come to be served, but to serve.'"

But even Jesus set His limits. When the crowd closes in around Him in Matthew 8:18 He gives "orders to cross to the other side of the lake." He had priorities, goals, and a mission to accomplish. He didn't simply do things because they were available.

4. *Concentrate on today.* Sydney J. Harris said, "The art of living successfully consists of being able to hold two opposite ideas in tension at the same time: first, to make long-term plans as if we were going to live forever; and second, to conduct ourselves as if we were going to die tomorrow."

Today is all we have. We never know whether it's our last. The jack of all trades has twenty tasks going at once, perhaps with none finished. The expert concentrates on one. He not only gets something done; he gets it done well and with a relaxed, happy smile on his face.

There's the old story of the farmer who went out hunting with his hound dog. When the farmer returned, he still seemed fresh, but the dog flopped down on the porch, exhausted. Someone asked him what was wrong, and he said, "Well, it wasn't the walking. We only covered ten miles. But there wasn't a gate open along the way that he didn't go in and examine the whole field. Not a cat appeared but that he had to chase it—rabbits, too. And there wasn't a dog barked but that he wore himself out barking back and showing fight. He must have gone fifty miles to my ten. No, it weren't the route that got him, but the zigzagging."³

I fear that the time crunch we feel is because of our zigzag life-styles. Instead, we must home in on the target and reach it.

ONE OF THE MASTERS

Satchel Paige, the great African-American baseball pitcher, was one who did that one job and did it well. Before breaking into the American League at forty-two, he pitched some 2,500 games in the black leagues, winning 2,000 with a remarkable 100 no-hitters. One year he played 153 games and started on twenty-nine consecutive days.

His first manager asked him, "Do you throw that hard consistently?" Paige answered with characteristic humor, "No, sir, I do it all the time!"

Dizzy Dean, the St. Louis Cardinal's master of disaster, once lost a thirteen-inning exhibition to Paige, 1-0. He said, "My fastball looks like a change of pace alongside that little pistol bullet Satch shoots up to the plate."

Paige was the king of pinpoint control. He could drive five nails in a board with ten pitches. At fifty-nine, he pitched his last three innings: one strikeout, one hit, no runs. His favorite quote was, "Don't look back. Something may be gaining on you."

Paige died at seventy-five in 1982. But his legacy lasts. He chose to be a master of one; and he ended up not as jack, but as king in the queen's court.⁴

A **tip on time:** What is one area of life in which you could consider yourself an expert? How do you think that figures in the spiritual, divine realm? Is it something that truly glorifies God? If not, then why are you spending so much time at it?

NOTES

1. William Barclay, *The Gospel of Matthew* (Philadelphia, Pa.: Westminster, 1975), p. 280.
2. Noted in *Bits and Pieces*, May 1980.
3. Quoted, ibid., December 1978.
4. *Sports Illustrated*, June 21, 1982, p. 9.

Part 4

The Battle Can Be Won

23

Conclusion:
Take Time to Dance

Teach us to number our days aright,
that we may gain a heart of wisdom.

—Psalm 90:12

Bell Laboratories has discovered something marvelous: the femtosecond.

What's that? It's the thinnest sliver of time ever. In a single second light zaps forward 186,000 miles, more than halfway to the moon. But scientists now can fire a burst of laser light that lasts for 30 millionths of a billionth of a second. During a femtosecond, light travels less than the thickness of a human hair.

Imagine having to get a job done not in days, hours, minutes, or seconds, but in femtoseconds!

Yet, I have to admit, as I've observed how fast the guy behind me hits his horn when the light turns green, it may be within the realm of possibility!

HOPE FOR THE HARRIED HURRIED

Just the same, I want to encourage you to press on rather than pass out. Paul touched on the concept when he said, "Forgetting what is behind and straining toward what is ahead, I press on toward the goal to win the prize for which God has called me heavenward in Christ Jesus" (Philippians 3:13*b*).

Paul offers us three important pieces of wisdom about time, life, and destiny.

First, forget what lies behind. You've had a rough time? You've made mistakes? You've squandered your time? You've made wrong or poor choices? *Forget it!* Put it behind your mind. Confess it, if that's necessary, and then leave it back there where it belongs, safely entombed in that place which God says is as far as the east is from the west.

Part of the reason you have a time crunch, or you've made mistakes, is so that you'll learn from it. Planet earth is a giant laboratory where God is preparing us for an eternal reign in heaven. Examine your mistakes. Study them. Confess them and learn from them. But don't fret over them. God will never bring them up—in the angels' presence, in Jesus' presence, in your mother's presence, or in yours—ever again! So forget them.

Second, strain forward to what lies ahead. The word means to "stretch out,"[2] like a runner does as he burns down the track toward the tape. Push forward. Get ready for the opportunities that God will yet bring your way, and strain toward your meeting with them in time and space. God has great plans. So race forward to greet them with open arms.

Third, press on toward the goal. What goal? Winning the prize that God longs to award you in heaven! To "press on" means to run forward eagerly in order to lay hold of something.[3] In other words, go after the prize for all you're worth. Don't give up. As Paul said in another verse, "Therefore, my dear brothers, stand firm. Let nothing move you. Always give yourselves fully to the work of the Lord, because you know that your labor in the Lord is not in vain" (1 Corinthians 15:58).

TENDER, LOVING CARE

Peter Drucker, one of the great secular writers on time management, has said, "Everything requires time. It is the one truly universal condition. All work takes place in time and uses up time. Yet most people take for granted this unique, irreplaceable, and necessary resource. Nothing else, perhaps, distinguishes effective executives as much as their tender loving care of time."[4]

If executives look at it that way, how much more the child of God!

Howard Hendricks, a Christian spokesman on the subject of management and time, summarized his own feelings about it this way: "[the crush of time] has given me a greater sense of urgency. I saw the change occur when I turned sixty and realized I don't have eternity in which to make my impact for the Saviour. Only a little slice of time. Psalm 90:12 is my gyroscope. My wife and I sat down and determined a focused set of goals. We ask, if the Lord gives us ten to twenty more years of life and ministry, how can we spend them the most productively in terms of the limitations of time and energy?"

That is the question we all must ask.

But the answer isn't just plan better, set clearer goals, make up to-do lists, and set priorities. It's also *press on*. Keep on moving out. Don't give up. Don't worry about what's past. Set your eyes on the things ahead. As those opportunities to serve, love, give, and conquer come your way, take them with bold, unhurried strides. God Himself will give you the time to do right and glorify Him in the midst of it.

But there is something else, perhaps even more important.

FOOTPRINTS

I always think of that story of the footprints. A man dreamed he was walking on the beach through a storm. He saw two sets of footprints side by side: his and the

Lord's. But at certain points in the sand, when storms rained and hailed on them, the two sets disappeared and only one remained. The man was aghast. He asked the Lord, "Why weren't you with me at the most severe moments?" Jesus answered quietly, "Those were the times I carried you."

It's a beautiful image.

VARIATION ON THE THEME

But perhaps we might change the story slightly to relate to the problem we all feel with time. Now imagine you and the Lord Jesus walking down the road together. For much of the way, the Lord's footprints go along steadily, consistently, rarely varying the pace. But your prints are a disorganized stream of zigzags, starts, stops, turnarounds, circles, departures and returns.

For much of the way it seems to go like this. But gradually, your footprints come more in line with the Lord's, soon paralleling His consistently. You and Jesus are walking as true friends.

This seems perfect, but then an interesting thing happens: your footprints that once etched the sand next to the Master's are now walking precisely in His steps. Inside His larger footprint is the smaller "saintprint," safely enclosed. You and Jesus are becoming one.

This goes on for many miles. But gradually you notice another change. The footprint inside the smaller footprint seems to grow larger. Eventually it disappears altogether. There is only one set of footprints. They have become one.

Again, this goes on for a long time. But then something awful happens. The second set of footprints is back. And this time it seems even worse. Zigzags all over the place. Stops. Starts. Deep gashes in the sand. A veritable mess of prints.

You're amazed and shocked. But this is the end of your dream.

Now you speak. "Lord, I understand the first scene with the zigzags and fits and starts and so on. I was a new Christian, just learning. But You walked on through the storm and helped me learn to walk with You."

"That is correct."

"And I understand when You and I began to walk side by side. I see that then I was learning to walk with You in stride."

"That's true also."

"Yes, and when the smaller footprints were inside of Yours, I was actually learning to walk in Your steps. I followed You very closely."

"Very good. You have understood everything so far."

"Then the smaller footprints grew and eventually filled in with Yours. I suppose that I was actually growing so much that I was becoming like You in every way."

"Precisely."

"But this is my question, Lord. Was there a regression or something? The footprints went back to two, and this time it was worse than at first."

The Lord smiles, then laughs. "You didn't know?" He says. "That was when we danced."

My Goal

If there is a goal of this book, it's this: that time will not be an enemy. You can use it well. You can use it to God's glory.

Oh, there will still be deadlines, more dead than alive. There will still be those impatient husbands stomping around downstairs while you put the last finishing touches on your makeup and make him late for the dinner date. There will still be those long lazy afternoons that seem to end so soon.

But there will also be something else.

248.4
L781

97204

Yes—plan, make up your to do list, use your appointment book, kill three birds with one minute. Get organized. Double up. Triple up. Make the "most" of the opportunity. Give, love, reach out, get some space, find a few moments for yourself. Yes, all of that.

But a few things more. As Solomon advised us in Ecclesiastes:

Enjoy life.

Enjoy God's gifts.

Enjoy the Lord Himself.

And sometimes, when you and He are alone, when you feel grateful, full of love, caught up in that moment of joyful worship that only the Christian can know, in those times . . . dance.

DANCE!

NOTES

1. See *"epekteinomai,"* William F. Arndt and F. Wilbur Gingrich, *A Greek and English Lexicon of the New Testament* (Chicago: U. of Chicago Press, 1957), p. 284.
2. See *"dioko,"* ibid., p. 200.
3. Quoted in *Bits and Pieces*, December 1980.

Moody Press, a ministry of the Moody Bible Institute,
is designed for education, evangelization, and edification.
If we may assist you in knowing more about Christ
and the Christian life, please write us without obligation:
Moody Press, c/o MLM, Chicago, Illinois 60610.

3 4711 00148 5350